An A[ngler's]

Flyfisher's Odyssey

Seeking a Life of Drag-Free Drift in the Land of the Midnight Sun

Daniel P. Hoffman

with a foreword by Kelly Bostian

sweetgrassbooks
an imprint of Farcountry Press

ISBN: 978-1-59152-293-5

Maps © 2021 by Dave Highness/ASYNC GIS

About the cover art, which elements are used throughout: A rainbow trout completed in traditional Alaskan Athabascan Indian seed-beads, sewn onto tanned moose hide. Accents of sun and shoreline reeds completed in porcupine quills. Original beadwork sewn by Gwendolyn Hoffman.

The badge on the book's cover reflects the author's commitment to donate 50 percent of his profits from the sale of this book, for this and all future printings, to Trout Unlimited in support of their Alaska operations. TU's Alaska staff, members, volunteers, and partners work strategically to help ensure that fish and their habitats are maintained for future generations to use and enjoy. Learn more about Trout Unlimited's work in Alaska at www.tu.org/project/alaska/

an imprint of Farcountry Press

Produced by Sweetgrass Books; PO Box 5630, Helena, MT 59604; (800) 821-3874; www.sweetgrassbooks.com.

 Produced and printed in the United States of America.

24   23   22   21   1   2   3   4

This book is dedicated my parents—
William and Phyllis Hoffman.

They raised me to be a fisherman.

Contents

FOREWORD

Alaska is spirit as much as it is water, woods, tundra, rock, and ice. The land beckons and beguiles those whose thoughts dare turn to the North.

If you are a flyfisher, God help your soul.

But if you truly love fly fishing, the inevitable experiences and the joining of your spirit with The Great Land will reveal that God has blessed you beyond measure.

Good fortune already is yours if you've laid hands on this book and turned to this page.

You now stand ready to feel swift water test your footing, all senses tuned with the river, your hand growing weak, your forearm burning, fly rod bent toward breaking, and soon a living torpedo, cold, slick and hard as ice itself, will allow your hand to ease underneath, lift, unhook, and savor a lifetime in a moment.

From the time of the earliest humans and through enduring Alaska Native culture, the turmoil of the rushes for gold and oil, no human has survived or enjoyed the best of what this land offers without the aid of good storytelling and good friends.

You would do well to get to know Dan Hoffman, a guy I knew mostly when I was outdoors writer and then editor of the *Fairbanks Daily News-Miner* and he was an experienced police officer and then Chief of Police.

Newshounds and top cops are seldom recognized as kindred spirits— quite the opposite. I like to think our shared backgrounds in the rhythm and pace of fly fishing Alaska's backcountry benefitted our professional relationship and, by extension, our community.

In my twenty-three years I was a mere tourist in comparison to Dan, who was already fly fishing at the age of twelve, when his family moved to the state and he never left.

He is imbued with that Alaska spirit and the storyteller in him—and perhaps some of his past experience as a fishing guide—knows how to share those ties in a way that others can feel it, taste it, see it and, perhaps, put it to good use.

If the spirit moves you, if you've been beguiled, if you wish to again hear that sweet spirit's whisper tugging at your heart, then read on my friend, read on.

—Kelly Bostian
https://kellyjbostian.substack.com ◎

INTRODUCTION

This book was designed to be bound and covered in a manner similar to a well-worn bible, and that is by intention. However, in the spirit of full disclosure, I do not wish to embark upon this journey under a flag of false pretense. While I was dutifully raised in a strict Catholic household, even serving as an altar boy for a time, I've rarely darkened the door of a formal church gathering as an adult. Nowadays, when my aging fingers seek the balm of holy water, it's not found within the confines of a small, golden basin. Rather, it swirls about my wrists and forearms in both comforting and hypnotic fashion, providing its own gentle blessing as I sift through a stream's stony cobble in search of larval clues.

I've read that an increasing number of people now commonly identify themselves as *SBNR: Spiritual, But Not Religious*. This designation rings rather true for me, as the majority of my contemplative time is spent trying to make sense of this world and my purpose within it. Is there truly some omnipotent and benevolent force out there artfully setting the course of life's currents as they drift throughout the universe? While I've been casting about in close proximity to that particular overhanging branch for quite some time, I have yet to wrap my line firmly around it. If there *is* such a presence—and he (or she) has watched me fish—then they must surely have one hell of a sense of humor. That said, while I'd like to think I've figured out a few important truths thus far in my nearly sixty-year journey, I suffer no illusions in believing that I'm anywhere close to achieving total enlightenment. Of one thing, however, I'm absolutely certain: For me, there is no better place to try and piece these mysteries together than upon the flowing waters of a small trout stream.

Now please bear in mind, I am well aware that I'm not wading into virgin waters here. A litany of excellent writers (including Babb,

Gierach, and Lyons to name but a few . . .) have all sought to frame the complex issues of mindfulness, ethics, and even mortality within the context of man's angling pursuits. However, that does not deter me from exploring and relating my own metal ruminations. Some of my finest—and arguably proudest—days on the water have been spent carefully working my way down a stream, following directly behind another party of skilled fly fishermen.

While the contours of the drainage, depth of its crossings, and barriers of bordering vegetation may have dictated that I follow in their general path, my approach to any specific shelf, riffle, or hole has always been my own. Maintaining trust in my observations and perceptions, while selecting tactics based upon my own accumulated knowledge and experience, has often allowed me to pick off several fine fish immediately behind the group that had already passed through. And while it most assuredly reflects a fundamental flaw in my character, I'll readily admit that I take a decidedly perverse amount of pleasure in achieving such an accomplishment . . . all the more so when I can see the rearmost member of the group stealing upstream glances with increasing frequency, shaking their head in frustration at the prizes they had missed. Infinitely more satisfying, though, is when that trailing member pauses, flashing a knowing smile and perhaps offering a brief, respectful nod, before continuing on.

We know.

—Daniel Hoffman
December 2020, Fairbanks, Alaska ◉

For Bob —

So glad to make new friends with wonderful people like you at Kulik!

I hope you enjoy the book —

Keep on fishing!! ☺

Best —

Dan Hob

Kulik Lodge
Sept 23, 2022

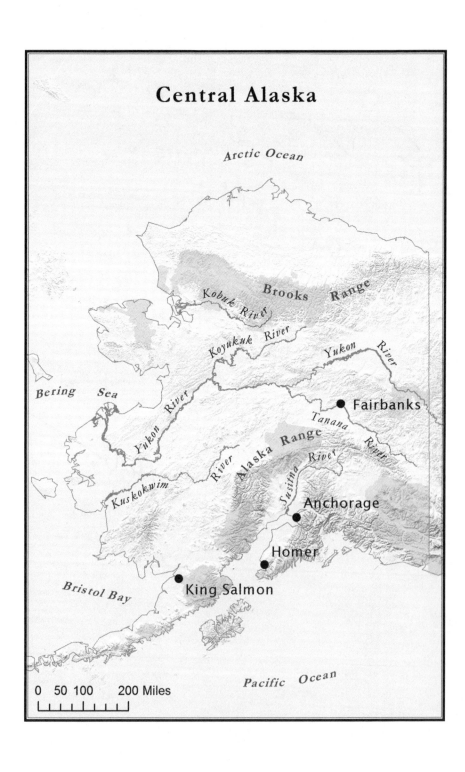

Central Alaska

Arctic Ocean

Brooks Range

Kobuk River

Koyukuk River

Yukon River

Bering Sea

Yukon River

● Fairbanks

Tanana River

Alaska Range

Susitna River

Kuskokwim River

● Anchorage

● Homer

Bristol Bay

● King Salmon

Pacific Ocean

0 50 100   200 Miles

PART ONE

In Search of Flowing Waters
The Seasons of Alaska

Chapter One

WINTER

I t has been said that absence makes the heart grow fonder. As the frozen stillness of Alaska's Interior sinks into a pool of ever-increasing darkness, my thoughts of a flowing, fishable trout stream have become both intoxicating and torturous. Water is rarely wet here at this time of year; it covers most of the landscape in a layer of hoary and bone-dry insulation, the accumulation of which can vary widely from one winter to the next. In some places, a thin layer of frozen crust may cap the snow's surface—a lasting reminder of a brief October warming trend that won't repeat itself 'til mid-April. In other spots, compaction due to wind or other activity will create a solid base of freeze-dried Styrofoam, where the pronounced squeak of one's walking will increase markedly in volume as temperatures head south of forty-below.

The rivers in our area have been locked up tightly for many weeks now, with entire stretches of smaller streams freezing predictably solid. In a somewhat cruel twist of irony for dog-mushers and other winter-time travelers, the sudden appearance of lethally wet "overflow" can sometimes spring forth in sinister ambush. Here, the very deepest pockets of water—having thus far remained insulated and slowly flowing under winter's protective cover—finally fall victim to the weight of accumulating snow and ice overhead. As this crushing mass pushes downward with determined and inevitable force, the water has no choice but to escape via any available path. With the solid floor of the streamed

supplying no viable alternative, it squeezes upwards through cracks in the ice. If prospective travelers are fortunate, the water will continue through the uppermost layers of snow, whereupon its flow will falter as it slowly glaciates, building layer upon layer of a highly slippery, yet thankfully visible, hazard on the trail.

Far worse, the most insidious of overflow will sometimes fail to breach the snow's top layer. Dependent upon temperatures and the timing of subsequent snowfalls, a thin, false icecap may form over the top of the newly liberated stream. Water now continues to flow over a base layer of ice, while remaining hidden under an insulating —and dangerously concealing—new layer of snow. For those travers-ing the wilderness at thirty- or forty-below, finding one's snowmachine or dogsled suddenly punching through the uppermost layer of snow and sinking into a liquid morass provides a sickening rush of fleeting insanity: free-flowing water simply *cannot exist* in these conditions! Or, at the very least, has *no business* doing so. (And yes, I said "snow-machine;" anyone this side of the 60th Parallel who uses the word "snowmobile" is clearly a southern tourist!)

Luckily, I have no such hazards to contend with on this early winter's day. It's morning, and I'm in desperate need of some coffee. As I set off towards the kitchen in my routine and pre-caffeinated stupor, I can just start to make out the beginnings of a faint glow on the southern horizon. It's actually more of a tentative, atmospheric promise than that of any discernible daylight, with a slowly expanding blush that seems to defy gravity as it bleeds upwards at a deliciously languid and maddeningly indifferent pace. While a forgotten sliver of last month's November moon still remains inexplicably suspended in the southern sky, nearly all remaining stars have now retreated into the impossibly dark-blue expanse at the uppermost edge of my view.

It's nearly 10:30 a.m., and the sun still remains stubbornly hidden below its scheduled point of emergence. Far to the south at this time of year, its bashful, sloping trajectory has now sufficiently backlit the towering silhouette of an ever-present legion, dutifully rising to guard the Tanana Valley's southern flanks. Predominantly white when seen in full daylight, the currently featureless, black barrier dominates the landscape as an imposing, monolithic wall. These colossal ramparts of granite, snow, and glacial ice comprise the mountains of the Alaska Range, with its paramount sentinels of Hayes, Hess, and Deborah standing resolute watch over the slumbering city of Fairbanks.

Denali, somewhat aloof in its placement at the far western end of the range, is still firmly ensconced in darkness. As North America's tallest peak, this massive general won't assume its vigil until early afternoon. There, it will stand in solemn observance as the fiery orange and yellows of a sustained, low-angle sunrise yield all too quickly to the soft, salmon pastels of an extended midwinter sunset. During these shortest days that bracket our northern solstice, the sun will trace a hopelessly shallow arc as it crawls just a few degrees above this mountainous horizon, with the entire panoramic progression lasting less than four hours. Laughingly mocked by the tilt of earth's axis in this "land of the midnight sun," December provides a scant amount of sun, while dishing out generous portions of midnight.

Another nightly stretch of extended darkness will inevitably follow. But, in a possible conciliatory gesture, the sun now offers its most surprising and wondrous contribution. Perhaps aware that the holidays are fast approaching, and surely aware of the shipping deadlines imposed upon distances exceeding ninety-million miles, emissions of charged particles sent forth from solar flares have ensured the timely delivery of a billion small parcels, cheerfully dropped at the front porch of Alaska's

upper atmosphere. As this multitude of tiny gifts accelerate through our planet's magnetic field, their collision with gas molecules will emit the shimmering and hypnotic palette of greens, purples, and glowing whites comprising the *Aurora Borealis*. Clear skies will ensure maximum visibility, providing a spectral show of northern light that's often bright enough to illuminate the vast, snowy expanse below. I live in a dreamworld.

Back to my coffee. It's exceptionally cold down in the valley this morning, and I don't bother to check our outdoor thermometer to confirm my observations. I've lived here long enough to accurately gauge the cold through a combination of visible and auditory cues, one of which was provided before I managed to drag myself out of bed. As I lay snugly next to my wife beneath two of her handmade comforters earlier this morning, I heard the first of the regularly scheduled *Wright's Air* Navajos pass over the house, returning from the village of Fort Yukon or Tanana as it gradually began its descent towards Fairbanks. A twin-propeller airplane sounds distinctly different from their single-prop brethren, and both can be easily distinguished from turbine jet engines. However, whether a specific type of aircraft hums, buzzes, or roars, each has its own unique sound-profile, and they all resonate with a perceptively sharper crackle and pitch when passing through extremely frigid air.

"Shit," I whispered to Gwen, ". . . it sounds cold out this morning."

Throwing on some sweatpants and shuffling down the stairs, my view to the south immediately confirmed my suspicions. The plume of steam visible from the city's central power plant rose only a short distance skyward before bending sharply to the right, falling back slightly before flattening out to form a suspended, wispy ceiling over the majority of town. Where the lights of civilization (I might argue that word later . . .) could be seen through the translucent haze, sharp and distinct columns of skyward illumination were captured within the fog's suspended ice crystals. These ghostly beams further confirmed the presence of extremely cold air, as this level of pronounced refraction doesn't occur when temperatures are warmer than minus-thirty or so.

While the power plant's horizontally flattened plume confirmed that the city dwellers were trapped within a folded quesadilla of frigid air, foul moods, and car exhaust, the column's pronounced bend—occurring well below the level of my own vantage point—conveyed and confirmed a phenomenon that I'm often privileged to enjoy throughout these midwinter months. Our home is perched atop a crescent-shaped ridge a few miles north of town, and the nearly thousand-foot gain in elevation provides a benefit that rivals its expansive southern view. The predominant stillness most commonly seen in the lowlands combined with the settling of cold, denser air, results in consistent temperature inversions throughout the worst of the winter, often resulting in ridgetop temperatures twenty to thirty degrees warmer than those experienced on the valley floor.

"Time to trim the banana trees . . ." I smiled and muttered to myself, as I found a bit of creamer in the back of the fridge.

While I suppose it may simply reflect an amalgamation of adapted coping mechanisms, reveling in these small thermometric victories while getting lost in the sublime beauty of winter's frosted stillness and low-angle light, my current existence comes at no small cost. I'm a fisherman. Scratch that; I'm a *fly fisherman,* and predominantly a stream flyfisher at that. And while Alaska has truly provided the stuff of my fly-casting dreams, particularly in the pursuit of trout, grayling, and salmon, the absence of flowing waters for several months each year has proved that nature can indeed be more than just harsh mistress; she can be a truly indifferent and cold-hearted bitch.

I've lived just outside of Fairbanks for nearly forty years now, and my wife was born here. As a fisherman, I've started to perceive this

expanse—and my own measure of time—with a somewhat skewed perspective, much in the same manner as folks who earnestly discuss the relationships with their beloved pooches in terms of "dog years." While it's conventional wisdom to assign a one-to-seven ratio for such canine calculations, I figure that a roughly four-to-twelve ratio (reducing down to one-to-three; thanks Mrs. Arno . . .) realistically reflects the limitations of the four-month, fishable season that currently occupies my annual trip around the sun. Now, I'd like to think that such a modest and reserved outlay of time and effort on the water would keep me roughly two-thirds younger than that of my angling contemporaries to the south. However, in a somewhat shocking turn of events, things don't seem to be turning out that way. Many of my friends in the Lower 48 seem to be getting in a lot more fishing than I do, while I continue to age in the same manner that I always have.

Thankfully, this hasn't been too big a problem over the past few years, as my life's accumulation of marketable skills and assets have finally allowed me to dance around the outermost fringes of the more economically well-endowed. Gwen and I have always prioritized the need for travel, particularly during the winter months. Through a combination of her warm and compassionate understanding (and my incredibly subtle application of psychology and campaigns of sustained whining) some of our tropical retreats have now been combined with a stop at a cold-water stream destination along the way. I've recently been able to extend my regular fall season through the entirety of October, visiting Colorado to chase rainbows and browns on the streams of my early childhood. We've also visited and fished some exceptional trout waters in both New Zealand and Patagonia during Alaska's midwinter, providing a level of seasonal escape that definitely bears repeating.

With everything finally coming up roses, I left my job in early 2020 to join my wife in full-time retirement, already plotting and scheming the course towards our next prospective fishing destinations. I suppose I should've predicted that it would only be a matter of time before a worldwide pandemic reared its ugly head, halting all non-essential travel and mandating that responsible folks "hunker down" for the coming winter. Luckily, when it comes to adopting marginally anti-social behavior, most of us Alaskans are already well ahead of the game. If staying inside one's own home, where niceties such as hosted cocktail parties (or just wearing pants, for that matter . . .) need not be observed, I can guarantee that I'm up to the challenge.

For now, I'll strive for contentment by donning enough layers to hike, skate, and ski in all but the very coldest of temperatures. When the mercury can no longer be coaxed from its baseline reservoirs, I'll work on inside projects, stopping to tie a few flies when I need a break from my more mundane chores. I'll help Gwen in the kitchen as we enjoy the bounty of moose and salmon that sustains us throughout the year, and we'll watch more than our fair share of movies in the evening as we gaze over the sparkling lights of Fairbanks below. I'll do all of these things as I continue to eye the southern horizon, waiting for the snow and ice to release their soul-crushing grip on my home waters. Hopefully, it won't be too much longer . . . at least not in "Dan years." ◉

Chapter Two

SPRING

It was the best of times; it was the worst of times...
—**Charles Dickens**, *A Tale of Two Cities*

t's a great quote, but I'll come clean: I never read the entire book.
However, the fundamental discord reflected in this simple, introductory phrase left a powerful impression upon me, as it fully encapsulates the torturous dichotomy that defines an Alaskan spring. The book itself did once manage to provide me with a somewhat more practical and useful platform; I'd photoshopped its cover to reflect *A Tale of Two Dinners*, providing an illustrative accompaniment for a rather pointed letter I'd penned to Alaska Airlines. (Helpful hint: Should you ever be offered their "chef-inspired" turkey dinner, I'd suggest taking a hard pass. . . .)

In my efforts to set a properly somber and dignified, literary tone, I began my missive with the appropriate preamble:

> *It was the best of meals, it was the worst of meals, it was the age of air travel, it was the scourge of coach, it was the epoch of hunger, it was the epoch of incredulity, it was the season of Alaskan winter, it was the season of Costa Rican summer, it was the Texas barbecue of hope, it was the Alaska Airlines meal of despair . . .*

Luckily, the corporate staffer who received my correspondence seemed to genuinely appreciate my highly expressive efforts, as I waxed poetic while dissecting their culinary abomination in extreme detail. I suppose my letter may have provided a momentary distraction, and perhaps a welcome departure, from the angry and profanity-laden complaints that most airlines are likely to receive. As someone who apparently shared my sense of humor, and perhaps as a literary kindred-spirit of sorts, the agent graciously refunded the cost of our meals, along with providing a noteworthy credit for future travel. As airlines go in general, Alaska Air is among the very best. (Turkey dinners notwithstanding.)

But I digress. . . . While not claiming to have full knowledge of the author's narrative with respect to that particular tale, the "best of times/worst of times" phrase has always stuck with me. Dickens apparently possessed a good understanding of the fundamental duality that could exist within circumstances, accompanied by the conflicting emotions that likely result. Accordingly, it leads me to believe that Charles ("Chuck" to his friends up here . . .) surely must've spent at least one springtime in the far northern latitudes of Interior Alaska.

As conceptual divisions of time go, defining spring as a true, full-blown "season" constitutes a bit of a stretch when one finds themselves north of the Alaska Range. Don't get me wrong; in terms of sheer import and overall transformational significance, there is no time of year that Alaskans greet with more frenzied excitement and anticipation. While these are indeed "the best of times," the issue—or perhaps more of a sticking point—is one of proportionality and delayed gratification. If placed within the analogous timeframe of a yearly holiday calendar, one can define the week of Christmas through New Year's Eve as a timespan roughly equivalent to that of a highly anticipated Alaskan summer. After enjoying a brisk New Year's Day, (which qualified as autumn in its entirety, in case you missed it . . .) you now spend the remainder of the year scraping frozen windshields, guarding against frozen pipes, and shoveling snow. Spring?

Well, that would be represented by the stunningly short interval of Christmas Eve, when all of the giddy children eagerly await Santa and his sleigh-load of promised presents, too excited to fall asleep in anticipation for what they know to be coming.

Within some contexts, such a characterization may be a bit of an exaggeration. For those enjoying outdoor winter sports, the spring season can be considered to start a bit earlier, ushered in by the combination of gradually warming temperatures and (of significantly greater importance) the inevitable increase in daylight. As Fairbanks lies less than 200 miles south of the Arctic Circle, we gain only a couple of precious seconds of light per day immediately following December's winter solstice. Those small, incremental gains don't seem to add up to much, especially as one begins the long, slow slog through January and February. (And while the latter is technically the shortest in terms of calendar days, on a psychological basis it consistently proves to be the longest month of the year.)

Ahhhhh . . . but then there's March! The additional seconds have continued to accumulate, and as a function of the earth's orientation and position in its yearly orbital journey, the daily gain in daylight now begins to accelerate at a noticeable pace. Through the latter part of the month and on into April, we'll experience an addition of several *minutes* of sunlight per day, the difference of which is no longer subtle. This seismic shift in daily illumination now provides a significant mood-altering lift, as workers and students suddenly notice that both ends of their daily commute are no longer shrouded in perpetual darkness. This is the time of year when cross-country skis get their glide back, and when snowmachine trips become more a function of seasonal enjoyment, rather than one of perpetual cold-weather endurance and subarctic survival. We all know what's coming, and Santa's sleigh can't get here fast enough.

13

Unfortunately, I'm a fly fisherman, and that brings us back to "the worst of times." While I'm as appreciative of the growing daylight and warming temperatures as anyone, it now only serves to heighten my impatience and frustration. Rivers and streams will remain frozen and covered with snow for several more weeks yet, and I take little comfort in knowing that the travelers who follow the creek's trails are enjoying the last of their springtime journeys. It'll still be quite some time before breakup. In years of particularly mild conditions, "ice-out" won't occur on the major drainages of the Yukon, Tanana, and Nenana Rivers until very late April; in most years we'll be waiting until May. The fishable, clearwater tributaries of the Chena, Salcha, and others will jealously guard their winter's covering parka even longer, as the larger down-stream rivers must first open up and flow, eventually providing a path-way for the smaller streams to finally shed their loads of ice.

The month of May can best be described as "true spring" for the Interior Alaskan fisherman, in all of its frustrating glory. Streams will now begin to flow, though they'll likely rage and churn in high, murky runoff for a few additional, maddening weeks. Midterm conditions will depend primarily on the depth of the winter's accumulated snow-load, as springtime precipitation is rarely a factor. May is often one of our driest months in terms of precipitation, thankfully hastening the thaw of remaining snow and returning area streams to their status as beckoning, fishable gems.

Water may be starting to flow in the country, but it seems to be backed-up to a standstill everywhere around town. Many of the subter-ranean storm drains remain tightly frozen, in desperate need of a steam truck's attention. The largest lakes in Alaska, ones such as Illiamna, Becharof, and Tustumena—may temporarily lose their crowns to the new record-holders, as whitecapped reservoirs suddenly occupy the intersections of Airport Way, Cushman Street, and the Old Steese

Highway. As the snow continues to recede from yards and alleyways across town, the discarded and long-forgotten detritus from the previous fall emerges in defiance, prompting a desperate need for cleanup. Such tidying chores may prove to be difficult; many areas are protectively surrounded by the emergence of several layers of frozen dog shit, accurately chronicling a record of the past winter's successive snowfalls in the same manner that tree rings can be counted on a freshly cut stump. Now basking and thawing in the springtime sun, the preponderance of turds will add their own odiferous funk to the seasonal potpourri of the Far North.

Luckily, I won't be fishing anywhere too close to town. In true Alaskan fashion, the landscape in which I find myself is once again the product of stunning, visual transformation. The watershed valleys that define the boundaries of my local explorations are most commonly dominated by a combination of dwarf birch, alder, and Labrador tea in their higher reaches. As stream waters tumble to the lower valleys, they slow to eventually meander through broad stretches of poorly drained muskeg and black spruce bog, bordered by willows and interspersed with boreal stands of white spruce and a mix of birch, aspen, and poplar.

If you're used to carrying a compass in the woods, you needn't bother here. South-facing slopes receive the lion's share of sun and are thus quicker to thaw and are inevitably better drained. The leaf-bearing deciduous trees dominate these expanses, showing a clear demarcation from the north-facing forests of spruce. These sharp divisions bisect all surrounding ridgelines, providing a clear signpost for geographic orientation.

An inspection of low-level flora upon the sunbaked microclimates of the uppermost, south-facing bluffs of the Yukon and Tanana river valleys reveals remnant populations of sage and dryland grasses, stubbornly clinging to their Pleistocene origins. Their presence serves as a surprising reminder of Northern Alaska's prehistoric past, where far

warmer temperatures hosted the presence of mastodons and steppe bison as they grazed along semi-arid plains. One thing's for sure: The pre-ice-age climate would've provided me with far more fishable months . . . saber toothed tigers be damned!

No longer on the lookout for woolly mammoths, I now bear witness to an impressive display of explosive synchronicity, as the budding leaves of area birch and poplar burst forth in coordinated and instantaneous fashion in the hills surrounding Fairbanks. This extraordinarily sudden transformation marks the area's highly anticipated "green-up" day, usually occurring by May 15th. While some of the less fortunate souls in the area can be seasonally derailed by the nearly crippling pollen counts that result from this over-the-top, seasonal explosion, I luckily have a high tolerance for such conditions.

Perhaps the most significant harbinger of the coming summer season is realized via the appearance of one of our most noteworthy residents: the ubiquitous Alaskan mosquito. The first wave of this annual onslaught can be easily handled, as the lumbering and drunken members of spring's first generation arrive to hover slowly and clumsily overhead, looking to score their first warm-blooded meal of the season. It's the second and subsequent generations that I'll need to mentally prepare for, as these smaller and considerably faster swarms of deter-mined kamikazes will prod and pester without mercy 'til the first frosts of autumn.

Nearing the end of the month, I'll finally be prepared to transition into the three official months of summer: June, July, and August. May can still prove to be a real wildcard; it might well be snowing on us at mid-month, or it could already be soaring into the mid-80s, causing the first "red flag" fire warnings of the season. I'm uncontrollably antsy at this point, and I'll find any excuse to seek the season's earliest, fish-able water. While I can always find nymphing water in the latter part of May, if I'm able to start catching grayling on any dries by month's end, I'll consider the spring to be "successfully average" within its yearly progression.

It's relatively easy at this time of year to quickly gather up my gear at a moment's notice, as I've had the entire winter to get things purchased, replaced, cleaned, patched, repaired, lubricated, categorized, stocked, organized, tied, wound, staged, sorted, hung, deflated, prepped, and ready. The side of my office dedicated to my tying bench and its adjacent closet would do any small fly shop or sporting goods store proud, and the portion of my garage reserved for rods, boots, waders, and nets stands ready for immediate access. (Get back to me at the end of fall, and I'll let you know how things are looking then. . . .)

Gearing up for my first exploratory foray of the season, I'll need to prepare myself for battle. Regardless of temperature, long sleeves and a neck cover will be the order of the day. I'm careful to confine the application of mosquito repellant to the backs of my hands only, in preparation for a quick smear around my face and neck. Any contaminating application carelessly applied to the fronts of my fingertips— or palms of my hands—would inevitably transfer to my fly line and monofilament tippets, with disastrously corrosive results. If the bugs are particularly bad, I'll use the dope having a much higher percentage of DEET, though I absolutely hate the stuff. I have no doubts that the nauseatingly greasy, plastic-eating crap will inevitably prove to be cancerous, but I'm resigned to its use. We're on the cusp of summer, and I have fish to catch . . . ☉

Chapter Three

SUMMER

I've been banking my excitement and energy for nearly eight months now, and Mother Nature's balance is finally coming due. For those who've never experienced the feelings that accompany a Northern Alaskan summer, they're perhaps best compared with the exuberance of a teen's first unsupervised road trip, where a full tank of gas and a few cans of squirreled-away beer beckon towards a highway of limitless possibilities. Released from the shackles of darkened confinement, Alaskans will now seek to cram a year's worth of soul-wringing, exhaustive enjoyment into an intensive, hundred-day campaign of joyous and continuous outdoor activity.

I don't know what time it is . . . and frankly, I don't care. In marked contrast to the solar depravity of our winter's paltry efforts, the sun of our summer sky now boasts a roughly 340-degree procession, sliding beneath the northern horizon in the shallowest of dips for only a few dusky hours. Chirping robins and mournful thrushes can be heard at all hours, at least partially masking the ever-present hum of mosquitos. It's light outside pretty much all of the time, providing one less factor to consider when planning a day's—or night's—adventure.

As with many of our seasonal extremes, the specter of constant daylight is both a blessing and a bit of a curse. It can be tough to fall asleep (or to even realize that one's supposed to *get* sleepy) in the complete absence of any nocturnal cues. The continuous state of illumination can be a bit disorienting to outsiders, providing some predictable comedy as we observe the arrival of new summer tourists. The plaid-pants wearing, blue-haired crowd is now walking among us, having apparently followed the annual migration of America's waterfowl north-ward. (Sporting, in remarkably ironic fashion, their own goose-down vests as they emerge from air-conditioned buses, hopelessly overdressed for the Interior's 80-degree summer weather.) Arriving daily from Alaska's southern ports, these wandering adventurers are dutifully puked forth from their cruise- ship motorcoaches to bask in our constant day-light, remaining blissfully oblivious to the passage of time. We'll watch in bemused detachment as they scramble about tirelessly into the late-night hours, ultimately crashing in complete and inevitable fashion as their accumulated expenditure of energy finally outweighs their bodily reserves.

As a more knowledgeable local, I simply can't afford to waste any of summer's precious time as a wandering zombie. While I'll justify the minimization of sleep to the greatest extent possible during these weeks of high-octane activity, a certain amount will be necessary to fuel my campaign of extended streamside exploration. Planning accordingly, I'll transform our bedroom into an appropriate summertime sanctuary. While a cooling fan may be necessary to facilitate my rapid departure into dreamland during these surprisingly warm nights, blackout shades are the top priority. If for some reason they're not available, a layer of tinfoil applied to the window will do just fine. It seems crazy when I stop to think about it, but for at least a few hours each night I'll long for the return of winter's comforting blanket of darkness.

In another display of mind-numbing contradiction, I'll find myself occasionally cursing the very sun I'd been yearning for a few short months ago. Why? Because the damned, ever-present sunshine initiates an accelerated and sustained period of ridiculous, hyperactive growth for any and all manner of vegetation. While this thrills our local gardeners to no end, cultivating beautiful flowers and producing amazingly large vegetables to a degree that astonishes the tourists, for me it simply represents the starting gun for the encroaching jungle's race to surround and engulf my home.

I'll admit it, I'm not much of a yardwork, exterior-maintenance kind of guy. When it comes to a choice between going fishing—versus mowing, weeding, and brush-cutting for the day—you should be readily prepared to start packing our lunches while answering my questions regarding recommended tippets and prevailing hatches. Predictably, my avoidance of such chores results in our home adopting an appearance of increasing neglect and abandonment as the summer months progress, which chafes at my otherwise orderly nature. If only the grass were to grow during winter when all of our streams were frozen, I'd be *happy* to mow it!

In spite of my occasional bitching, I'm still firmly entrenched in the pro-sun camp. My little sister Diane lives in the small coastal town of Ketchikan, located at the southern tip of Alaska's Panhandle. Ketchikan receives up to 160 inches of rain per year, earning it the dubious distinction as our state's wettest city. Making her living as an accomplished musician and keyboard entertainer, I've often asked how she manages to work her piano's pedals while wearing swim fins. Perhaps she'll eventually answer in one of her letters, which I'll likely have to throw in the microwave to dry out before reading.

Why do I fixate upon the sun and the rain? Because they provide the single most significant factor in determining the status of our Interior summer on a scale of livability and—more importantly—the fate of my fishing season. As a general characterization, our Interior summers are known to be hot and dry. The protective, curving arch of the Alaska Range blocks much of the moisture from the Pacific Ocean as it spirals and spins-off northward from the Gulf of Alaska, leaving the Interior to bask in relatively low humidity with a high degree of sunshine. Most of our summertime rains will follow the patterns common to inland regions elsewhere on the continent, where clear mornings often give way to the steady afternoon buildup of towering cumulous clouds on the horizon. Thunder, lightning, and sometimes intense showers may follow, with a return to clear skies by early evening. Given the millions of acres of forested lands that surround us, the lightning can pose a big problem.

With most sincere apologies to those in the western U.S. and elsewhere who've been adversely impacted by the recent spates of destructive wildfires, I'll readily admit that I'm actually quite fond of the faint, acrid tang of smoke blown in from distant, burning forests. A shift in June breezes will often find it seeping into my consciousness, providing an almost ever-present backdrop that (at least for me) defines the very essence of an Interior Alaskan summer. I suppose I developed this affinity in my teens, as I'd traveled north from Anchorage during the summers of my high school years to spend three transformative seasons at a Youth Conservation Corps residential work camp, located 30 miles outside of Fairbanks. Laboring to build hiking trails in the Chena River Recreation Area, the pronounced change in climate was a welcome relief from the damp, dreariness of Anchorage, where forest fires were rarely a concern.

Upon coming north, the noticeably deeper-blue skies and warmer temperatures of the Interior instantly brought feelings of both vitality and comforting familiarity, reminiscent of the Colorado mountains that I'd grown up in 'til the age of 12. While the common presence of wild-fire smoke was a bit disconcerting at first, it soon embedded itself into the hard-wiring of my brain as an integral component of life in the Far North. After graduating high school, I decided to attend the University of Alaska-Fairbanks; I've remained in the Interior ever since.

Such nostalgia notwithstanding, over the course of the intervening decades we seem to have become firmly entrenched in an increasingly "either/or" model of devolving summertime conditions. Either we receive *way* too much rain, swelling streams to unfishable levels, or we spend the summers cloaked in a suffocating mantle of excessive wild-fire smoke, courtesy of the local lightning. The midsummer months of 2020 proved to be an extreme example of the former, as historically high levels of rainfall in the Interior drove me (somewhat paradoxically) to the southcentral coast in search of fishable conditions. I can't remember *ever* having seen such rains around Fairbanks, as the home waters of my favorite streams ran high, murky, and un-wadable through the entirety of July and August.

Conversely, the preceding summer of 2019 found me struggling to spot rise-forms along the smooth stretches of my favorite Interior creeks, as my eyes were frequently stinging when looking through a dense layer of smoky haze. I had to frequently wet-down my protective facial buff; I'd originally purchased it to guard against excessive sun, but now commonly used it as a filter against the thick, choking smoke generated from nearby wildfires.

I try to roll with the punches when it comes to the weather and other related conditions, as I've gotten better over the years at shedding stress over factors that I can't control. If nearby conditions are good, I'll probably fish here. If chased off by excessive smoke or high water, I'll go in search of fish elsewhere. The most valuable commodities that I've found in retirement are those of freedom and available time, where the confinements of daily or weekly work schedules no longer preclude me from the possibility of an impromptu road trip.

With all that being said, it's finally summer! I'll frequently be on the move in search of optimal waters, and the possibilities are dizzying. However, as a denizen of the Interior, I'm immediately constrained by a fundamental and primary choice to consider, the determination of which will dictate my budgeted allotment of time, fuel, and hours (or days) spent behind the wheel of my pickup. Do I want to fish grayling, or do I want to fish trout? While there are certainly myriad additional options that are frequently added to this list, (to include northern pike, sheefish, arctic char, lake trout, all five species of pacific salmon, and halibut) there are a few notable factors that consistently bring me back to this familiar and determinative fork in the road.

As you may have picked up on by now, the mountains of the Alaska Range play a pivotal role in my existence. While I've already addressed their importance as an impediment to both Pacific moisture and winter-time sun, the formidable chain serves as a barrier of far greater pertinence to my life as a fisherman: It marks the northernmost boundary of Alaska's rainbow trout distribution. Save for the lower tributaries of the Kuskokwim and the mind-blowingly rich drainages of Bristol Bay far to the southwest, (travel to either of which would require a significant allotment of time and hefty expenditure in bush air-travel) a quest for trout in flowing streams will necessitate southbound travel down the George Parks Highway. ("Highway Number 3" in D.O.T. parlance, though most Alaskans would be hard-pressed to correctly identify any of our major highways by number . . .)

Heading down the Parks to skirt the eastern flanks of Denali and continuing southward, I'll normally bypass the clearwater tributaries of the Chulitna for all but the briefest of windows in late August, when egg-seeking rainbows shadow the progression of spawning silvers and chums before immediately backing down into their silty, unfishable home drainages. I may head to a few key spots that I like to fish in the middle-Susitna's clearwater tributaries during the height of the July king spawn, tracking the presence of some broad and exceptionally dark-colored 'bows that I consistently find in the upper reaches of a particularly favorite creek there.

However, If I'm indeed headed south in search of trout, another destination is far more probable. If I have rainbows on the brain, I'll likely be headed all the way down to the rivers and streams of the Kenai Peninsula. A drive of merely five- to six-hundred miles, (dependent upon my most southerly target . . .) the journey is roughly equivalent to a quick trip from New York City to Raleigh, or a last-minute jaunt from Great Falls, Montana, to Salt Lake City. In Alaska, our distances tend to be defined more in terms of hours travelled rather than in miles. Luckily, I have the time to spare.

While I do love to catch rainbows, most are a LONG way from my home. I'm therefore quite fortunate to have a solid alternative in much closer proximity, saving dozens of hours of prospective travel time every summer. The silvery blue arctic grayling, perhaps best known for its oversized, sail-like dorsal fin, is my target of preference in the Interior. The answer to any flyfisher's most fervent prayers, the grayling perhaps best exemplifies all of the finest attributes sought in a gamefish. Requiring cold and pristine waters, grayling have remained plentiful here, while all but disappearing from most of their prior range in the northern and western portions of the Lower 48.

Voracious in their appetites and mercilessly predatory, the local grayling will serve me with a steady and sustained dose of fly fishing over the course of the summer. Perhaps more importantly, they'll provide me with a strong dry-fly inoculation, with continuous follow-up boosters as necessary, to balance the preponderance of streamer and egg-pattern fishing I'll do to the south. While nymph fishing can be highly productive, especially in the caddis-rich environs of my favorite home water, I'll rarely have the discipline to stick with it for long. My addiction to surface takes is simply too strong, and in a rather gracious display of symbiosis, the local grayling's topside gluttony will happily satisfy my own insatiable cravings.

I have several favorite grayling spots located within close proximity to town, (i.e., within an hour's drive . . .) and many others within a reasonable, half-day distance. My closest friends know which creek I'll be found on during periods of extreme heat and ultra-low water, as they know what defines my ideal day. I've also recently discovered a couple of "new," highly productive upland creeks that I'd never bothered to fish before; these will thankfully provide me with some additional alternatives for escape when extended rains swell the streams of our lower valleys.

Now that I no longer have to worry about showing up for a regular job, I invariably don't bother to plan my calendar to the extent that I used to. However, I can't be too careless with this trait during the summer. There are several annual, required pilgrimages necessary for insertion amongst my normal streamside ventures, should I wish to keep peace in our family. Gwen and I will need to head down the Richardson Highway (Alaska Highway #2, changing to #4 after Delta Junction) in late June or July, taking advantage of the Copper River dipnet fishery to secure our winter's supply of fresh sockeye salmon. We'll head even further down the Rich to the stunningly beautiful town of Valdez on at least one occasion to fish the ocean waters of Prince William Sound, as I have yet to successfully catch a halibut in any of our Interior lakes, much less pull a pot of fresh shrimp. A camping trip to Homer at the southern tip of the Kenai Peninsula will nearly always be on the list, and my primary moose hunt has been shifted back to a ridiculously early date in August. (Thanks to the shooter that I commonly split the moose with, and his residential status within a federal subsistence management zone near Paxson.)

As summer moves toward its inevitable close, Gwen will push for at least one trip to the Tanana Valley State Fair, passionately professing the need to secure our annual photo button. I'll protest, but will likely be more willing if a decent band has been booked. (One advantage of our advancing years: Most of the bands of our youth are now considered has-beens, with many touring the summer fair circuits at rock-bottom, bookable prices.)

Overall, it'll be an exciting, hectic, and exhaustingly pleasing summer to be sure, where the more humdrum tasks of everyday life will predictably fill the remainder of any available spaces. Temptations for travel to the Lower 48 for specific events may occasionally arise, but will rarely be acted upon. To leave Alaska in the summertime for anywhere— or ANYTHING—is nearly unheard of and may present cause for a clinical diagnosis. For now, the flowing waters of my beloved state will provide for yet another wondrous season of exploration, further filling the banks of my memory to a delightful level of overflow.

So many rivers, so little time . . . ☉

Chapter Four

FALL

Truth be told, it's somewhat difficult for me to even write this final, seasonal chapter. Autumn represents the most bittersweet of all transitions to be found in Alaska, echoing what I've come to recognize as a pattern of repeating, pronounced duality that defines my life in the Far North. The sudden appearance of shimmering yellows in the forests, combined with the astonishing transformation of upland hillsides into their fiery tapestries of crimson and gold, provides the most visceral and stunningly visual reminders that heaven is indeed a place upon this earth—and we are living in it. Fall is truly a wondrous time, yet its final, waning hours can be incredibly difficult to face.

As temperatures begin to drop, the nightly formation of crystalline ice along the edges of local waters immediately invokes a sudden, fight-or-flight response for those who live here. As the ice becomes more persistent, tentatively expanding its reach outward to the river's mid-channels, we come to grips with the inevitable realization that winter is but a few weeks away. Heavy frosts, hitting the low-lying basins first, will ambush those gardeners who tend toward procrastination, and those who don't have garages will scramble to find the windshield ice-scrapers that they'd casually tossed aside in the spring. The transition invokes both a profound love for the richness of the season, and a heartbreaking realization that our times of flowing waters are coming to their inevitable close.

Like so many other influences that have shaped my life, my intense love for fall as the most favorite of seasons was ingrained in the experiences of my youth. Growing up in the mountains of Colorado, fall was most closely associated with our family's annual deer-hunting and fishing trips. Traveling up to three hours to reach my father's favorite haunts in the southwestern part of the state, (the distance of which comprised an epic journey at that point in my young life) the excitement and wonder of those experiences were without equal when compared to the other activities of my childhood. Occurring within settings of cold, frosty mornings, brilliant blue skies, and the ever-changing palette of Colorado aspen, my distinct autumnal orientation towards the appreciation of life's vibrancy was born. For me, no other season comes close.

As is the case with spring in Alaska, fall can barely be quantified as a true season, particularly if one finds themselves north of the Alaska Range. Autumn's duration can be exceedingly brief—sometimes heart-breakingly so—dependent upon the weather in any given year. In general, for those of us living in the Interior, the month of September will usually qualify as autumn in its entirety. In the rarest of years, a protracted "Indian summer" will provide an extended period of sunny skies and warming daytime temperatures through the early part of October, bestowing an additional window of late season dry-fly activity that I'll shamelessly soak myself in. In other years, the snow that's received by mid-September will be here to stay for the duration of winter.

Autumn marks a time of extraordinary abundance, with residents invariably following the example of local Chickadees and squirrels as they scramble to locate and store their reserves for the winter. Close to home, potatoes will be ready for digging, and the crops of summer gardens will finally be ready for harvest. Cabbage, zucchini, broccoli, and spinach will all provide a tantalizing bounty—much to the delight of our local moose population, who'll blaze their paths of calamitous and pilfering destruction throughout the city and its out-lying neighborhoods.

Most of the accomplished gardeners here are exceptionally generous, willing to share a portion of their bounty with those having less-than-green thumbs. This is frequently done in barter for salmon or game meat, as the skillsets required to encompass all methods of full-blown subsistence don't often overlap. While those providing fresh vegetables are greatly appreciated, the repeated, anonymous deposit of orphaned zucchini upon ambivalent doorsteps should perhaps prompt a clue towards restraint in one's planting. One final note: If you've grown a bumper crop of Brussels Sprouts and are feeling generous, you can do me a solid favor by leaving them for the moose.

Venturing afield, the lure of wild berries presents yet another opportunity for intense, preparatory hoarding. While raspberries, salmon-berries, and currants are plentiful to the south, it's the pungent smell of fall's ripening cranberries (both highbush and lowbush) that provides the overriding, olfactory backdrop for Interior's autumn harvest. Slightly nauseating in its first fecal impressions, its peculiar odor somehow becomes increasingly satisfying as one wanders our birch-covered hills. One must set aside this particularly odiferous distraction, however, as another target of considerably higher prominence awaits in abundance. In Interior Alaska, the blueberry is king. Its tiny, green, paddle-shaped leaves will have often gone unnoticed throughout the summer, gath-ering sunshine and rainwater in a bashful and unobtrusive manner. However, as the air of early September rapidly cools, the leaves will now sport a bold shade of vermillion, carpeting the landscapes of both low-lying bogs and brush-laden uplands in a blaze of autumnal fire.

Tendrils and tangles of intertwined branches, having previously reached skyward with a cargo of green, un-ripened berries, will now droop sluggishly downward under the strain of their hanging, indigo burden.

Presenting yet another task in my list of mandatory, seasonal requirements, there'll be a spousal expectation for at least a couple of forays into our area hills, securing a sufficient quantity of blueberries for the coming year. Cleaned of excess leaves and twigs and spread in a single layer upon cookie sheets, the berries will be brushed with a very thin layer of sugar (to prevent sticking and clumping together) and frozen. This accumulated bounty of blue nuggets will then be stored in quart-sized freezer jars, ready for consumption throughout the winter.

I don't protest these berry-picking ventures for a couple of reasons: First, I recognize that the heavily laden bushes present a high level of attraction to our area's black and grizzly bears. While I have absolutely no desire to hunt these particular beasts in deference to their status as apex predators, I have no qualms in providing the requisite armed overwatch for Gwen, as her intense and directed focus will likely remain a few inches off the ground. Secondly, I've become increasingly fond of smoothies as a quick and convenient breakfast, with a concoction including blueberries, rolled oats, and peanut butter comprising my personal favorite. While I suppose store-bought blueberries could serve in a pinch, their deceptively large, water-swollen content doesn't hold a candle to the concentrated goodness of our local bounty.

While I've thus far emphasized vegetative concerns, don't get the wrong idea; I'm merely working my way up the food chain. One does not find a high number of vegetarians in Alaska, and the hunting seasons of fall underscores such a sampling. Moose and caribou are the most frequently sought-after game animals in the Interior, with a good-sized moose providing more than a freezer full of meat for the winter. There are wild bison to be had in a few specific regions, though the

Department of Fish and Game's raffle-style drawing permits required for such hunts have thus far eluded me. While a few friends of mine are diehard Dall sheep hunters, I'm convinced that the procurement of sheep flesh—in consideration of its overall caloric value—represents a net loss in total energy when tallying the significant expenditure required for a successful harvest. While I've packed-out more than my share of moose over the years, I haven't had to climb any 10,000-foot mountains to do so.

Of all the bounties that signify Alaska fall harvests, however, none is more centrally linked to our culture than that of our seasonal runs of salmon. Cohos (silver salmon) and chums (dog salmon) are generally the latest fall spawners, with chinooks, (kings) sockeyes (reds) and humpies (pinks) generally wrapping things up a bit earlier. All five of these species of Pacific salmon will die after returning to spawn in their native drainages, with their decaying flesh providing an ongoing source of protein and nutrients to enrich their respective home watersheds.

Following the courses of its largest of rivers, the Interior has historically hosted large runs of king and chum salmon, (with some other species to a lesser degree) returning to spawn in our region after making their highly circuitous journey from the Bering Sea. It can be somewhat surprising to see these fish show up so far inland, as their route must circumvent the formidable barrier of the Alaska Range as it follows an extended, clockwise arc around the mountain's western and northern boundaries. The placement of large fishwheels—traditionally constructed on a floating platform of logs and utilizing the river's current to rotate two opposing, trough-shaped baskets—can be seen continuously scooping fish along the banks of our region's silt-laden channels. The fishwheels have been utilized by subsistence users for decades and can be found operating along the banks of the Kuskokwim, Yukon, and Tanana.

There are a few places where one can sport-fish for salmon in the Interior, as the fish depart from the confines of their large, silt-laden highways to spawn in the clearwater tributaries of their birth. Kings can be targeted in the lower Chena as it flows through downtown Fairbanks to meet with the Tanana, and late-season silvers can be found further south on the Delta Clearwater.

While such opportunities exist to fish for salmon nearby, I've never had the heart to pursue them. Any salmon that can be glimpsed in the waters surrounding Fairbanks has already made an upriver journey of over 800 miles just to reach this point, transiting the Yukon, Tanana, and Chena Rivers respectively. Having eluded commercial fishermen on the open ocean, then dodging seals and beluga whales as they enter the rivers, they must finally avoid fishwheels, subsistence nets, bears, eagles, and anglers as they approach the terminus of their perilous journey. Banking all of this effort in the hopes of having sex just once before death, I figure I should cut them a break and leave them alone.

South of the Alaska Range, immense, black clouds of swirling humpies clog the mouths of oceanside streams as they stage for much shorter spawning runs. The largest of Alaska's king salmon push forward into the Kenai, with slightly smaller genetic variants of the same species heading up numerous other drainages. Impossibly large schools of sockeye flood the drainages of Prince William Sound, the Southcentral Peninsula, and Bristol Bay, providing a bounty of unbelievable proportion. Chums and silvers seem to fill in any available gaps, as the state's waters come unbelievably alive.

Having spent decades in Alaska, I've developed a somewhat strange orientation when it comes to salmon. Perhaps because they're destined to spawn and then die, I tend to view them primarily as a food source to harvest when fresh, rather than as a sporting, catch-and-release resource.

It's always a bit perplexing for me to see the late season, out-of-state angler proudly holding up a grisly, spawned-out sockeye as their "trophy" for a photo, perhaps ignorant of the fact that the garishly scarlet, humpbacked monstrosity cradled within their conquering grip is far past its prime, and serving out its final, desperate days before death.

Additionally, for any road-based, accessible stream found in Southcentral Alaska, the presence of salmon usually means people . . . LOTS and LOTS of people. I'll endeavor in subsequent chapters to try and best explain my orientation towards stream fishing and the peaceful, contemplative outlets that it provides. However, you'll be hard-pressed to find any section where I extoll the merits of having multiple pixie-spoons cast across one's line, or the wonder in witnessing the majesty and grandeur of a drunken midnight domestic as Joe-Bob tries to extract a weighted Russian River fly from the brow of his girlfriend. (The predictable consequence of which, incidentally, I posit to be the *true* origin of the word "sockeye . . .") If people are crowding a stream in pursuit of salmon, it's highly unlikely that I'll be found amongst them.

Why, then, am I spending so much time addressing our state's Pacific spawners? The answer is inestimably simple and can be conveyed in a single word: TROUT. For me, the seasonal arrival of salmon in our Southcentral and Southwestern streams doesn't normally carry itself as a matter of primary concern. Rather, it serves as a cue for the development of a secondary condition; one of infinitely greater import, as reflected in the slight expansion of my earlier declaration: TROUT EAT SALMON EGGS.

Much of the referenced migratory activity associated with our various species of salmon takes place during mid-summer. However, the most intense and notable egg-drops don't occur until fall, when the salmon finally reach the uppermost portions of their drainages to culminate their spawning activity. Drawn like moths to a flame, the prospect of millions of fresh, protein- rich eggs being deposited over the course of a stream's gravel spawning redds presents a temptation that trout simply can't resist. Following the salmon upriver, sometimes for miles and often into drainages that are relatively barren and devoid of fish throughout the rest of the year, the trout will patiently bide their time, awaiting the autumnal buffet that's about to be set.

As a consequence, I'll let the combat fishermen duke it out on the lower portions of a stream as they target the latest wave of fresh, incoming salmon. I'm far happier when stealthily creeping to a stream's upper reaches, searching for the telltale presence of the comparatively dark and wavering, ghost-like shadows that hang just below the pods of scarlet and green spawners. Fishing small egg patterns or beads, ever adjusting the diameters and colors to best mimic the predominant eggs in the water, fall trout fishing in Alaska will fill me with the experiences and memories necessary to last through the coming winter. After happily catching and releasing fish to a point of satisfaction, I'll invariably head back downstream. While I'll still try to avoid the salmon crowd to the greatest extent possible, I'll occasionally meet one of their members on the trail, who'll likely want to commiserate after seeing my salmon-free, empty-handed status.

"Couldn't manage to catch any, huh? You know, they're pretty thick down below . . ."

"Yeah . . ." I'll reply in feigned frustration, keeping my long-practiced poker face, "I guess it was just one of those day . . ."

Returning to my home in Fairbanks after the last-fling trout trip of late autumn, (which, by definition, will have entailed a journey of several hundred miles) I'll casually toss my gear to the far-flung corners of my garage and office, now standing in abject, slovenly display as a tribute to an entire season's worth of rushed departures, sleep-deprived returns, and the inevitable, cumulative entropy that results. I'll have

plenty of time to get things back in order over the coming months;
I suppose I could dive in tomorrow and start straightening things up
right away, but to do so would require admitting to myself that that the
fall season has finally come to an end. I don't think I can handle doing
that just yet. ◎

Part Two

Childhood and the Family Sales Job
A Bait-and-Switch Campaign
at its Finest

Chapter Five

EARLY STREAM SCHOOL

Brain researchers call it the "Proust effect," categorizing those instances where the brief whiff of a long-forgotten odor brings a cascade of vivid memories flooding forth. While I've focused my own writings upon matters of true importance, (primarily those involving flyfishing and other worthy, outdoor pursuits) famed philosopher and author Marcel Proust was apparently a bit more of an "indoor dandy." As researchers have related, the musings of Proust included a rather voluminous recitation of memories involving his aunt's old house and immediate surroundings, the decades-old recollections of which were reportedly brought to the fore of his consciousness by the odor of Madeleines. (Diminutive, shell-shaped sponge cakes that are apparently quite popular throughout France, to include Auntie's house.)

While I've never been to France, nor eaten a Madeleine, a quick glance at my waistline would tend to confirm that I'm a fan of most cakes in general. Furthermore, I'm not going to pass judgement on Marcel ("Mickey" to his friends up here) regarding the specific content of his memories, as any such recollections would certainly be involuntary when triggered. As to his choice to actually write about them? Well, that's a discussion for another time. What I *did* find interesting, however, is that scientists have indeed confirmed that smells are among the most powerful triggers of memory, due to the close proximity between olfactory processors and memory centers in the brain. While

I'd been intuitively aware of the power of smell to evoke memories for some time, I don't believe I'd ever experienced it to the extraordinary extent that I did when visiting my folks this past fall.

After spending nearly forty years in Alaska, my parents eventually retired back to their home state of Colorado, settling in the small town of Cedaredge. Located in the southwest part of the state, their home lies in the rain shadow of the Grand Mesa, providing a relatively dry and almost snow-free refuge in a landscape dominated by sagebrush, piñon pine, and apple orchards. Located a few miles off the main highway, yet within close driving distance to the Gunnison and Uncompahgre Rivers, they couldn't have picked a finer place spend their remaining years together.

It was mid-October, and I was enjoying a short interlude of comforting familiarity with my parents. I had come down to Colorado for a few days in an attempt to put off the inevitable Alaska winter, extending my fall fishing season as I pursued browns and rainbows on several streams in the area. As was quite common, I hadn't bothered to schlepp a lot of extra fishing gear through the airports when coming for the visit; I keep a spare set of waders and boots at my folk's place, and there are plenty of extra flyrods, reels, and nets available if needed.

As he often does, my dad was puttering around the garage as I worked to get my gear together for a following day's trek up the Gunnison. Dad has now reached the age where he can't really hike or wade rivers any longer, and I'd be making the trip by myself.

However, if for no other reason than to spend a bit of additional time together, (which I certainly didn't mind) he ended up rooting through several of his many tackle boxes as he worked alongside me, as if searching for some critically important item that would ultimately prove indispensable for my upcoming jaunt.

After a time, he reached into his faded, multi-pocketed fishing vest. The garment hung from a small hook that he'd screwed into the side of a standing utility cabinet, with an adjacent hook holding its twin version (save for the smaller size) that belonged to my mother. Pulling his hand out of the vest's breast pocket with a flourish, he pitched an item across the large workbench that I'd set my fly boxes on.

"Here you go, Danny . . . you think you might need to use a few of these?"

I caught the container with a quick reflex action, then stopped to stare at what he'd tossed to me. Knowing my Dad and his fishing vest, it could've been anywhere from five to thirty years old, though the white lid of the small, two-inch jar appeared to retain its original seal. One side of the container was covered with an immediately recognizable gold label, and the transparent curve of the jar's opposite side showed it to be full of pale, peach-colored orbs, (immediately judged to be 10mm in diameter by my highly practiced, Alaskan bead-gauging eye . . .) each having a slightly darker, amber spot on one side. Turning the jar gently in my hand, I once again looked at the familiar label: *Titan Natural Salmon Eggs.*

I chuckled along with my dad, as we both knew I hadn't fished with such bait for over forty years. And while I'm not sure what compelled me to do so at that moment in the garage, I removed the cap from that jar of eggs and breathed in their essence. If Dad had been holding a shovel at that point, he may as well have hit me over the head with it. I was immediately transported back to the waters of Quartz and Cement Creeks, eight years old and up to my shins in ten inches of water, trying to delicately plop an egg at the head of a riffle without catching a willow behind me. Dad or Mom would've been a short distance upstream or down, in close enough proximity to scoop me up if I were to fall in. The distinct smell of the eggs was captivating, and I later wondered

just how long I'd stood there as a string of vivid memories came flooding forth.

As a diehard fly fisherman, I'd love nothing better than to spin the mythology that I'd grown up fishing nothing but flies, competing with my older brother David as we lost ourselves amongst the clear mountain streams of Summit, Eagle, Gunnison, and Hinsdale Counties. While rivers did run through our lives in a profound manner, our realities and instruction were a bit more, um, *meaty* than those of the famously autobiographical MacLean brothers. (Though being the younger brother, I suppose it's my shocking and uncanny resemblance to Brad Pitt that draws the frequent and inevitable comparisons . . .)

My Grandparents fished with fly rods, my parents fished with fly rods, my older siblings fished with fly rods, and from the time I was old enough to tie my own shoes, I too would learn the art of fishing with a fly rod as my primary tool. The fact that we were taught to fish with a single salmon egg or worm, rather than a fly, seemed to be part of the natural order of things.

Further, even at my very young age, I took great pride in joining the ranks of *stream* fishermen, reveling in the complexities that flowing currents brought to the game. I largely followed my dad's lead in avoiding the lakeshores, where any moronic kid could be parked with a Zebco rod- and-reel combo and a packet of pink marshmallows.

I grew up as the third of four kids in a relatively low-income household, with my parents both working fulltime to keep us all clothed and fed. The fishing trips that combined with our deer hunts were not done so much as a measure of sport, but rather as a means of necessary augmentation to our larder. While several of my friends had fathers who also hunted mule deer, I was always fiercely proud of the fact that my mom was a crack shot and good hunter as well. Following one year's hunt and our subsequent family butchering-day ritual, I remember

Mom laying out a few dozen packages of freezer-wrapped venison on the floor in the detailed shape of deer, placing a small set of antlers on its "head" to take a picture. She would carry that photo in her wallet for years, invariably pulling it out whenever one of her exceedingly ladylike friends would ask how she could shoot such poor, defenseless beings. "Honey . . . when I look through the scope, this is what I see . . ." Mom would say. As an eight year old, it was pretty neat to have such a cool mom.

Hunting for mule deer on the sage covered hills surrounding Lake City or the Powderhorn was primarily a dawn and dusk activity; once the deer had bedded down for the morning, it was time to go fishing. While my brother and I had already gained some experience from our time exploring Vail Creek, the Ten Mile, and numerous other small brooks in the vicinity of our Summit County home of Frisco, it was on the waters of the Gunnison's Lake Fork where we received our formal studies in stream fishing at the hands of my father and mother.

As I'd said, we were all taught to fish using fly rods. Before being bestowed with a rod of my very own, I would use one of my dad's spares—usually an Eagle-Claw *Trailmaster* four-piece pack rod, possessing the necessary diameter and heft to haul up an Alaskan Halibut, much less an eight-inch Colorado brookie. One of my most exciting Christmases was experienced at the age of nine, when my older sister Donna and I both received matching fly rods and reels of our very own, joining the ranks of my older brother David as having our "own stuff." The standard rigging of our outfits was fairly simple: A lightly colored fly line of seemingly any type (and often dubious characteristics) was housed on a small reel. I'm pretty sure that my father would not realize until much later in life that these lines were actually produced in specific categories, such as floating, sinking, etc. The "automatic" reels seemed to be Dad's favorite, sporting a spring-loaded dial on the side, with a trigger extending forward under the rod's grip that would activate its retrieval mechanism. There was no "backing" wound under the line, as the concept would've struck my father as hopelessly optimistic and somewhat delusional. The fly line would end in standard loop knot, large enough to be readily seen from a few rod lengths away. A loop-to-loop knot would connect to six or seven feet of monofilament, terminating in in yet another loop knot. Connected to this last loop would be a pre-tied, snelled salmon-egg hook, whose seven-inch leaders came in packets of a dozen from the nearby Wright & McGill company in Denver. The small, golden hooks were of perfect size and design to gently pierce the surface of the light orange Titans, where the point would be gingerly guided under and around the curvature of the egg's skin to firmly secure it. Yes, we were fishing bait with "fly poles," and the rods would rarely see a fly until several years later.

Other than the red-and-white, golf-ball sized bobbers that were commonly used by lake fishermen, we had never heard of a supplemental strike indicator. The terminal loop of our fly line, closely watched as it slowly sank and drifted downstream, was the closest thing we had. We were taught to fish largely by feel, in a Czech nymphing, tight-line type of style. (As it turns out, Dad was somewhat ahead-of-the-curve amongst his snootier fishing compatriots, as I hope he now realizes.)

Once rigged, I was somewhat oblivious to the delicate dance that now ensued, as my folks decided who would fish where, and which kids would be assigned to each respective parent. In my earliest years, I was often sent off with Mom (with my siblings often in tow as well) as I imagined my dad needed a certain degree of "alone time" to retain his sanity along the region's flowing waters. In retrospect, I have to think that Mom likely needed the escape from us ever-clamoring kids to an even greater degree, though I never heard any streamside arguments ensue when the day's marching orders were being issued.

Luckily, Mom was no slouch herself, as her fishing capabilities matched those of her prowess as a deer hunter. I learned a lot from fishing with my mom; the way she'd gently rotate her rod's metal ferrules in her ear to lightly lubricate them with wax before putting them together was slightly (and delightfully) gross to this boy's youthful perception, and it surely facilitated the rod's takedown at the end of the day. My mother was very patient and would carefully map out a hole to show me where the trout would most likely lie before turning me loose. There were certainly more than a few days when she'd out-fish all of us, met with a sense of chagrin—and ultimate pride—on the part of my father.

As I got a bit older, I could tell that my skills and abilities as a young fisherman were improving, as I no longer needed to be constantly and intently supervised. The change was confirmed, as it became more frequent for me to be assigned to my father's oversight as we were being split up for the day. Fishing a stream with Dad was always special, as I felt that the two of us were sharing deeply conspiratorial secrets as he explained the finer nuances of currents, cut-banks, and holding water. While Mom was often granted the low-hanging fruit of the prime, well-defined holes, Dad loved to fish the riffles, and would delight in coaxing fish from other spots that were (to my yet unpracticed eye) of dubious prospect at best. I learned to fish the close and intimately tight waters of small, brush-choked side channels, and he schooled me in the importance of adding tiny split-shot above the egg-leader's loop when fishing larger runs.

Perhaps most importantly, in learning to send an egg downstream in a naturally flowing and unobtrusive manner, lifting my rod tip periodically to flip a developing belly of line back upstream when needed, Dad was providing me with my first important lessons in the necessities of achieving a drag-free drift.

Reflecting his beliefs in the power of both goal-setting and definitive reward, Dad had established a prize of paramount pursuit for each of us kids. As we'd sequentially grown and progressed to fish largely on an independent basis, he had decreed that the successful catch and cleaning of our first five trout—all accomplished entirely on our own—would result in the bestowment of our very own, leather-sheathed, fixed-blade fishing knife. While I can't necessarily speak for all young kids, I can only say that within the framework of my own existence, the prospect of jauntily sporting a sheath knife as a confirmation of one's (obviously superior) outdoor mastery inspired a quest of complete and total effort. My brother David, three years my senior, had been the first to fulfill Dad's five-fish requirement, lording his knife over me in a manner that would only inflame my passions further. Donna, a year younger than Dave, would soon follow in receiving her own coveted trophy.

When I finally reached an age of sufficient abilities and coordination to fish on my own, I pursued my quest with unyielding determination. I had begun to target a large boulder that broke the Gunnison's current a short distance from the cabin that we commonly stayed in when deer hunting north of Lake City. I could look down at the pool created by the stone's blockage from a vantage point on the hillside several feet above the stream, frequently glimpsing brookies dart out from beneath the concave curvature of the rock to grab some passing morsel before returning to relative safety. I would approach carefully, crouching to ensure that my shadow wouldn't betray my presence, as I carefully cast to the upstream margin of the current in order to carry my egg inward along the boulder's base.

When I hooked a fish, I'd draw it quickly downstream away from the rock to the tail-end of the pool, as I didn't want to spook the other fish present. I forced myself to stop, stow the fish in my creel, and hike a short distance back uphill to scout the sunlit run once again, waiting for the visible activity around the rock's margins to resume. It was these disciplined, determined efforts that ultimately allowed me to run breathlessly back to our cabin with that fifth and final trout in my creel, where I received the prize that'll forever remain as the most meaningful of my young life. ☉

Chapter Six
A LAKESIDE INTERVAL

As I look back on it now, my evolution as a fly fisherman followed a somewhat circuitous, if not comically absurd, path. Already somewhat set in my ways at the crotchety age of ten and sporting the grizzled and seasoned demeanor that only a sheath-knife wearing, brook trout catching kid could pull off, I figured I was well on my way to becoming a true fishing legend. Intensely proud of my family's stream fishing heritage, I had started to develop the first judgmental parameters of my own junior-angler's sense of elitism, where my perceptions of another fisherman's skills and abilities were largely dependent upon whether they used a fly rod or spinning gear, and whether they fished streams or still water. For the lake fishermen, I'd deduct further points for bobber fishing and/or the use of closed-face spinning reels. Lastly, I'd immediately disqualify an angler from any further consideration if they used jars of bright red salmon eggs instead of our natural looking peach ones, or—worse yet—any type of dough, corn, or marshmallows.

I fished eggs with my fly rod, and I had yet to own (much less use) any of my own flies. Sitting atop the rear counter of *Merrick's Sporting Goods* in Frisco, a seemingly endless variety of these furred and feathered masterpieces occupied the divided compartments of a large, transparent display case. I would occasionally peruse the selection with a sense of awe and wonder, as they represented a rarified stratum within my newly defined pyramid of angling elitism—one that I assumed I'd never attain. I had never run into a true fly fisherman on the small creeks that I commonly fished with my brother, and I had yet to see my dad pull any of his own flies out for use, though several always resided in a small container within his tackle box or fishing vest.

A segment of *The American Sportsman* or some such show would periodically catch my eye on the television, filling me with awe as they showed a skilled expert decked-out in impossible finery, making magically long, looping fly casts to pull in fantastically large trout. I didn't know who these people were or where they came from, but I was reasonably sure that they weren't breathing the same air as me. I could hardly imagine traveling to such exotic rivers as the Madison, Au Sable, or Beaverkill, and any such attempts I'd made at "real fly casting" had immediately flung my egg from its hook and towards the heavens, with my line predictably snagged in the highest of branches. Artificial flies may have danced and skittered around the periphery of my imagination, but they continued to hover just out of reach.

It's more than a little ironic, then, that my first real use of flies did not come at the end of my fly rod. Rather, it was incorporated into the terminal setup of a spinning rig. Perhaps more shockingly, these lessons would take place on the still waters of a lake, rather than in a stream's flowing currents. In what were to be my last young years in Colorado, my grandfather Bernard had finally retired from stream fishing, as he could no longer wade with confidence. He, along with my beloved grandmother Irene, had bought a small Winnebago camper, and they drove from Denver on a regular basis to take fishing and camping trips at Sylvan Lake—a beautiful, trout-filled gem that's nestled among the pine-forested mountains south of Eagle.

In perhaps a bit of a sexist selection common for the time, my grandparents would frequently pick up my brother and I to take on their fishing trips, leaving my two sisters at home. Once the camper was parked and leveled, Grandma Irene would set about with any and all domestic preparations, while Grandpa rigged rods for fishing. His setup was relatively simple and proved to be devastatingly effective. A standard spinning rod was used, with an open-faced spinning reel hanging appropriately below. (If I saw another kid grab a spinning rod and hold it with the reel sticking up on top, I'd immediately scoff at their cluelessness . . .) My grandfather had an affinity for the *DAM Quick* brand of reels, with their roughened, dull black metal finish—a preference that I'd carry forward for many years.

In order to provide the weight necessary to cast a fly, my grandfather would use inch-long, clear plastic bubbles; their hollow-core tube would be pulled out to fill the bubble with water before reseating, with the reel's line then being threaded through. Once strung, a small swivel would be tied to the end of the line to prevent the bubble from sliding downward. A monofilament leader of five feet or so would then be tied to the swivel, with a special, "Sylvan Lake fly" tied to its terminal end.

Thus equipped, my brother and I would be placed at appropriate intervals on the lakeshore bracketing my grandfather, and fishing could commence. The rigs we used allowed for exceptionally long, soaring casts, particularly once I got used to the subtleties of their motion. Slowly pausing at the end of my two-handed backcast, I learned to allow the weight of the water- filled bubble to load extra power to the rod's tip before sending the fly forward in a strong, looping arc. While I'd like to say I could repeat this process effortlessly and repeatedly, my earliest sojourns were marked by an uncanny ability to produce monofilament bird's nests of monumental proportion. My Grandfather, (and my Uncle Mike or Aunt Mary, who'd sometimes join us) all displayed the patience of the Biblical prophet Job as they'd come to my repeated calls for assistance, stopping to stare in wonderment at the intricacy of tangles I could produce in such a short amount of time.

Luckily, the frequency of these snarls started to decline as a I achieved a level of comfortable competence with my spinning gear. After allowing the bubble to sink for several seconds, a slow to medium retrieve of the sunken, flashy fly invariably provoked hard strikes from the decent-sized rainbow trout inhabiting the lake. There were a few occasions when I'd manage to out-fish my older brother, and the time that we spent with both grandparents was priceless. As an additional benefit, and perhaps as a small indication of a growing, introspective maturity on my part, these outings showed me the folly of my here-tofore growing "system" of subjective and judgmental rankings when it came to other fishermen. I now realized that fish were where you found them, and that the methods used by anglers in their pursuits were largely a reflection of their own teachers, and—as in my grandfather's case—physical limitations that couldn't be overcome.

My grandparents had already provided me with the greatest of gifts through their time, love, and patience. However, in terms of my own fishing evolution, the most profound contribution emanating from our trips to Sylvan Lake was to evolve quite organically, and by virtue of one of my grandfather's other most notable characteristics: He was cheap. As I'd noted, our fly of choice for these trips had been dubbed the "Sylvan Lake fly," and was used by us on an exclusive (and protectively secret) basis. Serving as a generic attractor pattern, the fly was long and slender, utilizing a 2X or 3X hook-shank. The body consisted of densely wound peacock herl, ribbed with a full-length wrap of gold, medium-width tinsel. Bracketed at its front and rear by several windings of sparse furnace-hackle, the resultant fly most likely mimicked large dragonfly and damselfly larvae, as well as small baitfish.

My grandfather, however, had a problem. The specific characteristics of the fly he'd discovered were not to be found among the standard offer-ings of local fly shops. Worse yet, the fishing buddy who had previously tied and supplied the flies to him apparently had both the predatory instincts and strong business acumen of an inner-city crack dealer. Once it was apparent that Grandpa was fully hooked, the dealer was looking to jack up the price . . . considerably.

In a move of both cunning genius and patriarchal generosity, my grandfather arrived at a solution that would kill all his birds with one stone: He would pay a nominal, one-time fee to enroll my brother David in some local fly-tying lessons, thus ensuring him a steady supply of made-to-order flies far into the future. While I didn't realize it at the time, this pivotal occurrence was perhaps the most significant development in my own evolution as a fly fisherman. Once my older brother started tying flies, I immediately followed suit in what was to become a rather immersive preoccupation.

Like most little brothers, I constantly looked to my older sibling to gauge what was cool, which activities were worth pursuing, and—it goes without saying—which of his treasured items and supplies were worth pilfering. As David's stockpile of fly-tying materials grew, I found that I had all that I needed to start tying my own flies whenever he wasn't around. Like most tiers, I started with the easy stuff, clumsily crafting large woolly worms and misshapen deer-hair streamers. As I gained confidence and dexterity, I began taking stabs at the smaller, dry-fly patterns that seemed to be referenced most often in the fishing articles I'd read, with tying instructions found in the assorted manuals that had accumulated on Dave's bookshelf.

Speaking of manuals, I'd be somewhat remiss in my newfound status of "cantankerous, aging man" if I didn't take a moment to rail against the ease with which today's aspiring fishermen and fly tiers can readily access technical information. Not only did I have to navigate constant, blowing snowstorms in my youth as I trudged uphill both to and from school, when I finally got home and reached my tying vise, there was no internet or online fishing forums available to guide my efforts. I learned to tie flies the old-fashioned way, (consarn it . . .) stumbling along as I haplessly attempted to follow the innumerable series of sequential, black- and-white photographs in Jack Dennis' *Western Trout Fly Tying Manual.* A prospective tier can now Google the words "YouTube + (any conceivable pattern)" and voila! A detailed, color video, shot in high-resolution with an accompanying narrative, will demonstrate how a specific fly can be tied from start to finish. I suppose it'll ultimately yield a more well-supplied crop of fishermen, but I doubt they'll gain the character that comes through forty years of trial-and-error and the slow, incremental accumulation of knowledge that accompanies such a process. Okay, rant over . . .

My time in Colorado was coming to a close, as my dad had announced in the summer of '77 that our family would be packing up in the fall and moving north to Alaska! As a 12-year-old boy who was highly preoccupied with all things wilderness- and fishing-related, I could hardly sit still for the next several weeks as we prepared for the big move. Prior to departing, I bore witness to a final event that would inevitably send me down the flyfisher's path for good.

In late August, just prior to leaving for Alaska, my father took us on one last, late-summer camping and fishing trip to Cebolla Creek in Colorado's Powderhorn Valley. We'd fished the creek often, as the nearby *Six J's* guest cabins served as one of my folk's favorite basecamps to hunt deer from in the fall. As usual, we were fishing our standard set-ups, drifting single salmon eggs down through the bends and riffles of the fairly small stream as we enjoyed a final Colorado outing under brilliant blue skies. I can't recall precisely what I'd been doing during the last afternoon, but for some reason I had walked—rodless—up to the spot where my dad was fishing, at the tail of a small pool that had formed just beyond a section of tumbling water.

My Dad turned excitedly as he heard me, frantically waving for me to come forward. As I got closer he motioned to the water, which had suddenly come alive with an ample swarm of medium-sized, black insects, buzzing back and forth across the pool's mirrored surface. I could start to see some corresponding fish activity, as my dad clumsily rifled through his vest pockets. He finally pulled out the only container of flies that he had. It was a cheap, K-Mart kind of thing—a small, pie-shaped plastic dish with a rotating top that allowed access to three or four subdivided compartments. Turning the dial, my dad found the closest thing he could in his rudimentary efforts to "match the hatch," a couple of bedraggled and somewhat forlorn looking Rio Grande Kings of unknown origin.

My father tied one on and gave it a short flip forward; nothing even closely resembling the graceful, arcing loops I'd seen on the *American Sportsman*. No matter; within seconds Dad was bringing in an energetic fish, which he excitedly exclaimed to be a brown trout once palmed into his creel. We'd been catching brookies most of the trip, along with the occasional rainbow, but the browns had thus far eluded us. I was mesmerized by the fish's dark spots and golden skin as it was cradled in my father's hand; I had rarely ever caught a brown, and I'd always considered them to be a bit more mysterious and somewhat exotic. Dad caught several more in quick succession, then handed me his rod to do the same. The excitement and total wonder of hooking a trout on the surface with a fly—a REAL DRY FLY—provided a rush of excitement that far exceeded anything I'd experienced up to that point. Further, it firmly cemented and capped the foundation of knowledge that my dad, mom, brother, and grandparents had all worked to cultivate and instill within me over the past several years.

The activity of the hatch ended as abruptly as it had begun, though it provided more than enough conversational fodder as we packed up

that late afternoon and began the long drive home. Once we'd finally arrived it was time to get a night's good rest, followed by the immediate and final preparations for our family's 3,000-mile trek northward. At the end of the week, my parents would be cramming themselves, four kids, a Labrador retriever, and a caged parakeet into the fully packed confines of our Chevy Suburban, pulling a small trailer loaded to the brim with boxes of housewares, clothes, and all other items of miscellany as we prepared to start the next chapter of our lives.

I was headed to Alaska, and I was a fly fisherman. ◉

Chapter Seven

MY ALASKAN EVOLUTION

My brother David—I can say with complete and honest objectivity—
is a pretty impressive guy. A standout cross-country skier for the
University of Alaska Anchorage, he met his wife Tiina (who'd come over
from Finland to ski for UAA as well) while pursuing his justice degree.
After graduation he started his career as a cop, and he was a pretty
damned good one. I entered a career in law enforcement as well, largely
due to his influence, after wrapping-up a wildlife biology degree at the
University of Alaska Fairbanks. While I'd eventually join the ranks of
the Fairbanks Police Department, I first spent a summer living with
Dave and Tiina at their home on the Kenai Peninsula, where I was set
to begin work as seasonal Fish-and-Wildlife Enforcement Officer with
the Alaska State Troopers. I had just completed the academy in Sitka,
and I was as green as any rookie could possibly be.

Dave was working as a police officer for the City of Kenai at the
time, and as I prepared to enter my field training in the adjacent town of
Soldotna, he pulled me aside for a conversation, saying something that
stuck with me through the entirety of my career:

"Dan, you're going to be training with a bunch of different guys,
and you'll probably figure out pretty quickly that there'll be two types,"
he said. "You'll meet some who might only have five or ten years'-worth
of experience, but they've been hustling, learning, and growing ever year.
You'll also meet the veterans who have fifteen—or even twenty—years

under their belt, but they've been living the *same year,* over and over, for quite some time." He then wrapped up his observations with this piece of summary advice: *"Make sure that you pay attention to the guys who are actually paying attention."*

His words would prove to be quite prophetic, as I would quickly come to recognize those in my profession who worked to constantly learn and evolve, versus those who comfortably settled into patterns of routine, familiarity, and stagnation. Upon later reflection, I came to realize that this salient point of advice applied to far more than just police work, and that its ultimate applicability pertained to my development as a fisherman as well.

It might sound a bit strange—and I'm not quite sure why I do it— but I frequently look to aspects of fly fishing as a means of providing meaningful analogies, perhaps in an effort to provide a greater degree of structural context in my life. My Catholic upbringing would tell me that pride is supposed to be sinful, but I take a lot of pride in being a decent fisherman. And I don't think that this sense of pride is necessarily in recognition of my current skillset; rather, it's in acknowledgment of the 50 years' worth of paying attention, learning, and adapting that has brought me to where I'm at today. I don't know that I could've ever developed in the same manner had our family stayed in Colorado; if one is going to evolve as a fisherman, Alaska is a hell of a place to do it.

When we first moved north in the fall of '77, it was to settle in the small, coastal town of Valdez. The Trans-Alaskan Pipeline System (TAPS) had just come online after three years of intensive pipe-laying efforts, allowing crude oil to flow from the oil fields of Prudhoe Bay, 800 miles to the north. The pipeline's terminus was located on the shores of Valdez's ice-free port, directly across the bay from town, where a nonstop procession of oil tankers would berth to fill up before heading south to California. My father would be managing the *Sheffield House* hotel at the edge of the town's small boat harbor, while my mom worked as a nurse at the local hospital.

Driving down the steep, winding grade from Thompson's Pass into Valdez on the final leg of our journey, we were completely immersed in dense, ground-hugging clouds and drizzle, which remained constant for the entirety of our first week there. Stepping out of our temporary (and somewhat sketchy) trailer-home on the morning of September 20th, I was completely awestruck as clear skies and sunshine revealed the towering mountains that completely ringed the town and surrounding ocean waters. It was an impressive sight to behold, confirming that we had landed in one of the most stunningly beautiful areas of the entire state.

Heading into winter, where I'd end up shoveling more wet, heavy snow than I care to remember, I'd have to wait 'til the following summer to begin my Alaskan fishing education. In those first few years in Valdez before moving to Girdwood—and ultimately to Anchorage—pink and silver salmon (both fished in the ocean, primarily with spinning gear) were the primary target of pursuit. There wasn't much trout water to be found nearby, and I was crushed to discover that an exceedingly high number rivers running through the state (many whose courses I'd excitedly traced and highlighted on topographic maps) were glacially fed. Such waters carry a high degree of suspended silt, (resulting from the layer of underlying rock that's crushed by the weight and movement of glacial ice) resulting in a milky, gray slurry that's completely unfishable.

Worse yet, I would come to find out that many of the clear-running creeks were nearly devoid of life as well, with nary a fish to be found. Other clear waters exhibited a stunning degree of seasonality, with fishable trout or char to be found for only a few short weeks each year, in conjunction with local salmon runs. This was all proving to be *very* different from the rivers and creeks that I'd grown up on; while the fish in Colorado had generally been much smaller in size, they could usually be found in a stream at any given time of the year.

Luckily, I didn't throw in the towel in frustration. Once I had a little more mobility in my high school years, I was able start exploring the clearwater drainages of the Kenai Peninsula and middle Susitna valley, both of which offered trout and grayling. This was where my real fly fishing education would start, much of it being either self-taught or learned in conjunction with my brother. While some of the fish we pursued were certainly different, (e.g., I had never seen an arctic grayling before . . .) it was comforting to find that streams flowed in pretty much the same manner, and that fish would be found in the same types of holding-water. Knowing how to read the water and then applying any newfound knowledge with respect to local food sources would be my key to achieving fly-fishing success in Alaska.

In my earlier years of exploration, it seemed that most of the drainages south of the Alaska Range were most effectively fished with large streamers (e.g., sculpin patterns, marabou muddlers, woolly boogers, etc.) until such time that the presence of spawning salmon dictated a switch to egg patterns. Following the spawn, one could continue to fish an incremental and faded spectrum of egg flies, reflecting the progression of the natural egg's appearance in the streambed gravel as they became increasingly washed-out over time. Very late in the season one could switch over to "flesh flies," mimicking the remnants of skin and disintegrating protein that washed downstream from decaying salmon carcasses.

It wouldn't be 'til I found my way into the Interior that I started to do a lot of dry-fly fishing. With many of the waters more closely resembling the clear, freestone streams of my youth, I was instantly more comfortable as I waded in search of grayling. The amount of aquatic insect life seemed to be much more prolific than those of the Southcentral waters, perhaps due to the considerably hotter summers. Caddis and mayflies abounded, and I would soon realize that the grayling inhabited nearly every creek, river, and lake throughout the North.

The presence of grayling in nearly all waters, even gravel-pit ponds, provided me with an opportunity to showcase my newfound proclivity for the sleek, fan-finned fish. In what was to be my final summer working at a Youth Conservation Corps camp outside of Fairbanks, I had arrived a week early at the behest of Steve Cook, the Camp Director, to help set up operations for the coming season. Approximately forty teens from towns and villages across the state would be arriving soon, where they'd be divided and assigned into work crews for the construction of hiking trails throughout the Chena River Recreation Area.

Steve and I were currently the only ones working at the facility, and due to some kind of bureaucratic mix-up we'd not yet received any of the monies necessary to purchase food for ourselves or the upcoming camp. Steve, whose tendencies towards frugality would've made my own grandfather proud, took his own limited funds on a food-run to town, returning with a large bag of instant pancake mix and several bunches of green bananas. I then proceeded to catch nice-sized grayling on a regular basis from the camp's pond and adjacent Chena River, finding the springtime fish to be particularly fond of olive woolly buggers when stripped in a rapid-retrieve manner. Our diet for the week— albeit one of highly predictable monotony—was secured. (Though to this day, I don't think I could ever stomach a dinner of banana pancakes and grayling again . . .)

By the time I was nearing my senior year of high school, I felt that I was achieving a moderate level of success in my development as a fly fisherman, as well having sampled what I thought to be a fair representation of Southcentral and Interior waters. I'd managed to catch grayling to the north, trout and char to the south, and a LOT of salmon

of every species to be had in between. However, to this point, nothing could've prepared me for the seismic shift that was about to occur in my Alaskan fishing universe: My discovery of Katmai.

You never know who you'll meet and how the most random chain of occurrences can end up impacting your life in the most profound way. Such were the events that I'd later ponder, looking back on my life as I prepared to wrap up my junior year of high school in Anchorage. I had made three really good friends while in school, comprising an exceptionally tightknit group that remains intact to this day. One of those guys—Dave Highness—was my primary downhill-skiing buddy. As such, I was a frequent visitor to his house (and vice versa) over the winter as we'd pick up or drop off each other in conjunction with school activities or ski trips to Alyeska. Dave's stepdad, Bill Duckworth, happened to be a regional administrator with the National Park Service in Anchorage. While Bill and I didn't necessarily have a lot of long, deep conversations, we got along together well, and he was aware of my penchant for outdoor work and upcoming plans to study wildlife biology.

One early August day in '82, having just returned to Anchorage from my eight-week stint at the YCC camp, I received a rather unexpected call from Bill. He had just returned from a Park Service liaison trip to Brooks Camp in Katmai National Park and Preserve, where a company called *Katmailand* operated a well-known fishing lodge as the park's sole concessionaire. (One of the company's three *Angler's Paradise* lodges in Katmai, to include Brooks, Kulik, and Grosvenor.) The lodge's manager had spoken to Bill, advising that several of their college-age staff were leaving to resume their fall studies in the Lower 48. He then asked if Bill could recommend anyone in Anchorage who'd be willing to come out for just a few weeks to fill in for the remainder of the season. Knowing that our senior year of high school wasn't set to begin for almost three weeks, Bill advised that he could get me on a flight out to Brooks the next day, if I was interested.

For those who aren't familiar with the Katmai region of Bristol Bay in the remote, roadless region of Southwest Alaska, it's profiled in detail in an upcoming "special places" chapter. For now, suffice it safe to say, I was HIGHLY interested, and found myself flying to King Salmon the next morning, where I'd transfer to an amphibious, *Peninsula Airways'* Grumman Goose for the relatively short hop to Brooks Camp on the shores of Naknek Lake. For those looking for the National Geographic version of Alaska, where brown bears constantly prowl the streams, catching their dinners from the scores of salmon found leaping impressively over flowing waterfalls, this was it. Moreover, the populations of rainbow trout inhabiting the waters are as consistently prolific, with an insanely-large "average size," as any found on earth. I was now the proverbial kid in the candy store, and the fishing gods had apparently granted me the keys to the kingdom.

Between housekeeping, kitchen work, camp maintenance, and any other assigned duties for the day, I could be found on the Brooks River during any and all available spare moments, catching rainbows of a size that I could've never even imagined in Colorado. Having a good length of backing on my reel was now a critical necessity, and it was here that I learned the methods necessary to hook—and more importantly, *land*— big fish. The power and size of the local trout were truly incredible, and it was somewhat frustrating to know that my Dad was currently toiling away at work in Anchorage, a mere 300 air-miles away.

It was with thoughts of my father while at Brooks Camp where I first came to recognize the true "division of privilege" that exists throughout much of Alaska's waters. Due to its remote nature, high cost of getting there, and very limited lodging availability, (or even available tent-site permits for the NPS campground there) relatively few anglers would ever have the opportunity, or the financial capabilities, to visit such a place. The same holds true for most of the other drainages in Southwest Alaska, where anglers face the choice of patronizing high- priced fishing lodges or mounting self-guided expeditions of considerable logistics and cost.

While this realization provided some degree of sadness in light of my own brown-bagging, blue-collar orientation, I also quickly recognized that a place as special as Katmai would've been quickly overrun and consumed, had it been located within the well-traveled confines of the Lower 48, or even connected to Alaska's own extremely limited road system.

My first three-week stint at Brooks was heartbreakingly short, but it provided for my employment through the entirety of the following summer, as I'd been offered the chance to return and manage the camp's store and fly shop. Being there for the entire summer season allowed me to expand my explorations and knowledge significantly, often fishing with the lodge's guides, and sometimes getting to fly or boat to other nearby drainages on my days off. This further season of experience set the stage for what was perhaps the ultimate job of my (or likely any) young fisherman's life, working as a fly-fishing guide at Katmailand's neighboring Kulik Lodge.

Guiding at Kulik provided my Master's degree in the arts and science of Alaskan fly fishing, particularly with respect to the pursuit of trout. From the salmon smolt migrations of early spring, through the meaty streamer fishing of midsummer and into the insane egg-drops of mid to late fall, the Kulik and other nearby drainages provided a level of fishing that I was concerned might truly spoil me for life. Luckily, I've found that the lessons I learned on the watersheds of Bristol Bay have transferred quite handily elsewhere—to include my visits back to

Colorado—where I now routinely catch fish that would've qualified as monsters in my youth.

In the late fall of my last season, I had the opportunity to provide the ultimate fisherman's payback. Sonny Petersen, the lodge's owner, graciously flew my father out from Anchorage to spend a couple of days fishing the Kulik River during the height of the sockeye spawn—with me as his assigned guide. I was now able to reciprocate at least a small portion of the priceless gifts that Dad had bestowed upon me so many years earlier. Helping him to read the water, tying on the appropriate patterns to use and coaching him in some "real fly-casting" techniques, each large rainbow that was joyfully brought to the net for a quick inspection and release cemented an intensively satisfying relationship of love and fishing mentorship—one that I had finally been able to reciprocate.

It's all about paying attention, taking advantage of opportunities when they present themselves, and the willingness to work and grow. This was confirmed to be true throughout my career, and it would continue to guide my evolution as a fisherman as well. I started out this chapter by saying my brother Dave was a pretty impressive guy; I suppose I should perhaps wrap this up by providing some qualifications for that statement.

Shortly after leaving Kenai P.D. in the early 90s to go to work for the Anchorage Police Department, Dave suffered a massive cerebral hemorrhage while training in their gym. We'd been sheep hunting in the true "middle of nowhere" just a week prior; if the blowout had happened in sheep camp, I would've likely had to quarter *him* up to pack-out. (Sorry; we both continue to share a cop's morbid sense of humor. . . .) Luckily, he was immediately rushed to Anchorage's Providence Hospital, where he underwent brain surgery within the hour. The doctors were able to save his life, but he was left with permanent and pronounced left-side paralysis, to include a completely non-functional left arm and hand.

Though his condition necessitated a medical retirement from police work, my brother was not the type to fold up and cry over these developments. Returning to live in Tiina's home country of Finland, Dave gained acceptance into graduate school, where he learned to speak Finnish while simultaneously earning his Master's degree in the study of social sciences.

Fathering two boys along the way, he continued in his studies, eventually completing his Doctorate. He's now in the process of finalizing a seminal textbook in his field of study, working as one of their country's leading social-science academics.

Ever the competitive little brother, I'm always quick to remind Dave that I received my degree in the *real* hard-sciences, free of the subjective interpretations found in sociology. What impresses me to no end, however, is the fact that he can still fly fish. He's learned to tie flies one-handed (I still struggle with two . . .), and he'll hold his fly rod in his teeth when necessary to strip and retrieve line. His adaptations to all facets of life have been extraordinary, and he's truly one of the guys who's "always paying attention." Whenever I feel like complaining about high waters making it a little more difficult for me to wade, or whine that my "fisherman's elbow" is starting to aggravate my casting, I remind myself that Dave is on my speed-dial.

I haven't had to call him yet. ◉

Chapter Eight
A KATMAI CONVERSION
Coming Full-Circle

N o waterfowl has ever landed as gracefully. As we dipped towards the mirror-like surface of Katmai's American Creek under an impossibly blue mid-July sky, the only indication that we'd finally reached zero altitude was the sparkling plume of water suddenly fanning rearward from the right pontoon of our DeHavilland Beaver. With absolutely no perceptible reduction in our speed or engine rpm's, *Katmai Air* pilot Jeff Moody continued to skim the surface, following the placid curvature of the American for nearly half a mile upstream before gently reducing the throttle. As the last remnants of early morning mist retreated upon our approach, we finally settled onto both floats, turning towards the lush green patchwork of reeds and willows framing the creek's western bank.

I'd been lost in my own thoughts for a good portion of the short twenty-five-minute hop from Kulik Lodge, as the distinctive drone of the Beaver's nine-cylinder radial engine was far more conducive to introspective thought than active conversation. My father was seated directly beside me, and I was hard pressed to read the scope of his impressions as we scanned the unfolding scenery through our respective windows. Getting ready to once again fish with my dad, it was hard not to think back on my youth . . .

It was 1974, and I had just celebrated my ninth birthday. Now I was going to drown, and I would never see my parents again. As the stiff rubber treads of my brand-new *Big Chief* hip-waders continued to slip and slide over the seemingly conspiratorial algal surface coating the rocks of the Gunnison's Lake-Fork tributary, I faced the grim realization of my impending death. With the river's audible roar flooding my eardrums, I struggled against the quickening current—instinctively aware that it was too strong for my puny, sixty-pound frame. In my panicked state of mind, however, I felt a grim and foolhardy sense of determination as I pushed forward into the deepening waters.

Up until a few moments earlier, I'd been engaged in the solitary pursuit of rainbow and brook trout, drifting an oversized salmon-egg through the deeper stretches of my favorite autumnal fishery. I had recently earned the most coveted prize of my youth: a small fixed-blade sheath knife, and I was eager to catch and clean my contribution toward that night's dinner. I was using my dad's one and only fly rod, grudgingly bestowed a few hours prior with his usual parting warning: "Don't wade past your knees, and for God's sake don't break my fishing pole!"

My right hand now clutched the smooth and lovingly-worn cork handle in a death grip, while the faded tan fly line hung impotently from the last guide on the rod's truncated butt section. The drooping line met the current and extended out into mid-stream, where my youthfully imitative and somewhat spastic attempts to deliver the egg—ala "fly casting"—had managed to simultaneously dislodge and propel the tip section of the two-piece rod. The swirling current created brief refractory slicks through the surface glare, providing intermittent and fast-moving windows into the river's greenish depths. Using these transitory portals to glimpse the line's sloping descent, I could barely discern the ghostly outline of the three-foot tip bracketed between two submerged boulders, its tail ferrule undulating up and down in a slow-motion gesture of purposeful admonition and disdain.

My youthful sense of logic—in retrospect—was quite simple. It didn't matter if I ended up dying in pursuit of retrieval, as my dad would surely kill me if I returned with only half of his rod. I summoned the courage to take another step forward; the crush of upstream water was already boiling up and spilling over the tops of my waders, soaking the crotch of my Levi's and sending an icy bath down to my bare heels, left mercilessly uncovered by my worthless and perpetually balled-up cotton socks. As I began to take what I suspected might be my final step upon this earth, I suddenly felt two strong hands beneath my armpits as Dad lifted me silently and swiftly from behind, taking several steps backwards and depositing me on the blissfully dry riverbank in one smooth, twisting motion.

"What in Christ's name are you trying to do, Danny, kill yourself?" he yelled; my tears welled up as I tried to talk through a trembling lower lip, motioning helplessly over my shoulder towards the incriminating trail of fly line stretching outwards into the river. Certain that I was still on a trajectory towards certain death, albeit now on a somewhat different path, I was somewhat confused as a warm and understanding smile crept across my father's face. Slowly shaking his head as he turned me to face the river, he placed a firm hand upon my shoulder as the other gently pried the rod from my nearly paralytic fingers.

Curling his pinkie under a small protruding lever of faux ivory and steel, Dad activated the spring-tension trigger of his prized automatic fly reel. The quivering metallic device began to hum and click as it retrieved the slack line, with the egg hook on the end of my leader predictably catching the rod tip's terminal eye in the process. I watched dumbfounded as the reel's rasping, rotating spool conducted its lightweight recovery, dredging the slender wand up from the river's depths and bringing it straight to us, as if shot from an underwater bow by the hand of God himself. If my father had merely walked up, parted the waters of the Gunnison, and strolled out to retrieve his rod, I don't think I'd have been any less impressed.

Over four decades had passed since my nearly suicidal rod-retrieval, and a lot of things had changed. I had thankfully ditched the legacy of rubber hip-boots, and I'd somehow managed to pack on enough weight over the years to keep me grounded while wading in all but the swiftest of waters. I was now quite comfortable and confident in fishing a wide variety of drainages throughout Alaska, and I relished the opportunities that presented themselves.

A lot had changed for my dad as well. While he still loved to get out and fish, he was no longer as steady on his feet as he once was. He got tired and cold a lot easier, and I was now the one that provided the cautionary reminders not to wade past one's knees when fishing with him. I'd had limited opportunities to spend time with Dad over the past several years, and I hadn't noted the magnitude of these changes 'til we'd met up for a brief road fishing trip in 2010. As Dad continued to drive past many sections of fishable water, it soon became clear to me that the idea of fishing had become more practical and appealing to him, rather than tackling the actual task itself. Whether through my own selfishness, or perhaps through some sense of idyllic optimism, I resolved to provide my father with the best—and quite possibly his last—backcountry fishing and wilderness experience available in Alaska.

As my folks approached their 50th wedding anniversary in 2011, I spent several weeks of internal debate trying to gauge whether they would truly be up for the relative challenges of such a trip. It was a predictably cold February day in Fairbanks when I made the initial call, delicately trying to discern whether they would prefer such an anniversary adventure over the more celebratory—and boringly standard—escapist fare to the tropics. I had also made the somewhat difficult decision to bluntly confront Dad's growing limitations, hoping that the excitement of preparing for such an outing might outweigh any hurt feelings or bruised egos in the process.

"So Pop, you've mentioned several times over the years that you'd love to bring Mom out to Katmai to see the bears and catch some big fish . . . what would you think about Gwen and I taking you out there for your anniversary?" I could immediately tell by his tone that he was *very* excited at the prospect, but I needed to make sure that he was going into this with his eyes wide open. I cautiously continued, "You know, it's not like you guys are getting any younger; it'd probably be a good idea to actually do this while you can still climb in and out of a floatplane. . . ."

Luckily, his response and enthusiasm had me making our reservations by that afternoon. As winter slowly transitioned to spring, I spent the next five months educating him via phone and e-mail on trip preparations and proper clothes layering, as well as explaining the past thirty years' advancements in synthetic undergarment and wader technology that he'd largely ignored.

I also spent quite a bit of time discussing his developing knee issues, blood-sugar monitoring, and other health-related concerns. Talking both directly with him, and working somewhat covertly through my mom, we worked on a very gradual and steady increase in Dad's regimen of walking, stretching, diet, and flexibility exercises. I could always tell by Dad's tone when he thought I was nagging him a bit too much; my standard response would be to back off a bit, while simultaneously e-mailing a few recent photos from *Katmailand's* website, showing the exceptionally large Rainbow and Lake Trout that had most recently been caught and released. This strategy of long-term preparation,

punctuated by seeds of piscatorial motivation, had resulted in our arrival on American Creek that picture-perfect July morning.

Our pilot snapped me back to reality: "Okay guys, your chariot awaits," he said. Jeff gently nosed the Beaver onto a muddy riverbank, flanked to the left by a stowed johnboat, and punctuated by two sets of meandering—and very fresh—Brown Bear tracks. Our guide for the day, Hunter Hutchinson, was immediately out of the plane and up to his waist in the nearly still waters, turning the craft tail-in for unloading. After tossing some initial gear to the bank, Hunter began prepping the boat and outboard jet for our journey upstream, while I assisted my wife and folks ashore.

As I stood adjacent to the plane and provided a firm shoulder for my Dad to place a steadying hand on, I couldn't help but smile as I walked him down the plane's float and onto the riverbank. Looking warm, snug, and slightly sausage-like in his new neoprene waders, his sense of childlike excitement was palpable as we loaded the boat and headed towards the fast, clear waters of the Upper American. It would prove to be a day like no other.

Late that afternoon—joyous, sunburned, and completely spent— we were back downriver on that same stretch of riverbank awaiting our pickup flight back to Kulik. To try and fully explain or quantify the day's events would be an exercise in futility, as superlatives such as "beautiful," "magical," or "perfect" would fail to convey the totali- ty of the experience. Watching my mother (an accomplished fly fisher herself), and my own wife (who's proved to be a very quick learner) catch and release a nearly endless quantity of Arctic Char and Rainbow Trout was special enough in its own right. Finding ourselves upon bright, sunlit waters amidst a prolonged hatch of Caddis led to a degree of sustained surface-feeding activity that I'd rarely experienced while previously guiding these egg-dominated waters. To try and selectively target the trout and char among teaming schools of bright red sock-eye, with an almost ever-present progression of curious (yet sufficiently cautious) Brown Bears trekking the opposite banks, made for a setting that was both blunt in its realism, and profoundly wondrous in its beauty and complexity.

But best of all, there was my father—taking it all in. Wading with cautious confidence along the shallow margins of the American's pea-gravel bars, he experienced everything that Katmai had to offer. To take a short break from our frenetic fishing was not a concern to him, as that meant sitting back for a moment to watch Mom catch *her* fish, or to take delight in a juvenile Brown Bear's latest awkward swan-dive, scattering crimson missiles in every direction. His biggest concern was that of a sunburn due to a forgotten ball-cap, and the only soreness spoken of that day laughingly referenced his right wrist and elbow—the result of perhaps one too many fish brought in for a quick inspection and release.

While the next few days would cascade from one memorable experience to the next, from watching the stately gathering of Brown Bears at Brooks Falls, to absorbing the misty grandeur of Katmai's Valley of 10,000 Smokes, to watching him leisurely troll a spoon across Nonvianuk's "laker-hole" for a nearly guaranteed hook-up, that one perfect day on the American will forever stand in my mind as the single greatest experience that I could have ever provided for—and shared with—my dad.

As we waited on the riverbank, I busied myself with breaking down our rods and prepping our gear for transport. I watched as my father kept looking wistfully back upstream, looking beyond the riffles and runs of that day's outing—perhaps far beyond, all the way back to the waters of his own youth. With a growing hum finally registering in my brain, I looked up to see Kulik owner Sonny Petersen set one of

his distinctively wasp-like Cessna Turbo 207s down upon the river, arriving to provide us with a slightly faster return trip back to the Lodge.

As I knelt to grab my knapsack, I felt a firm and familiar hand being placed upon my shoulder. Dad gave a squeeze—and I turned to find myself looking into a pair of tear-filled eyes, focused upon me with a hauntingly familiar expression. It suddenly dawned on me that these were not the eyes of my father; nor were they the eyes of any 75-year-old man. Rather, they were the awkward, slightly vulnerable, and eminently trusting eyes of a nine-year-old boy on the banks of the Gunnison, grateful to be sharing a perfect wilderness with the people he loved most. My father opened his mouth to try and say something, but no words would come. He could only manage to squeeze my shoulder again—with a bit more strength than I'd felt in quite a while—as he turned to take a last, longing look upriver. That suited me just fine. ◉

Part Three

Life . . .
and its Most Special of Places

Chapter Nine

FRIENDSHIPS,
and the "Go-To" Flies in My Box

It was a rather glorious morning on one of my favorite Kenai Peninsula streams, as the mosquitos were both uncharacteristically (and pleasingly) absent. This was a damned good thing, as I currently found myself sitting buck-assed naked along the banks of the creek's gurgling waters. Perched somewhat precariously atop the only dry, moss-free boulder that I'd managed to find in the immediate vicinity, I marveled at the complete lack of biting insects as I luxuriated in the warmth of the early-August sun. And . . . before you go jumping to any conclusions . . . let me assure you that I'm *not* some kind of posy-sniffing, granola-crunching nudist.

If my presence were to be suddenly discovered, any competent streamside detective would quickly surmise my situation. Draped across the span of every available alder within arm's reach, one could see my wrung-out assortment of socks, lightweight polypropylene long-johns, and overshirts, all strategically positioned to catch the maximum amount sunlight. My small chest-pack, having thankfully retained its two fly boxes and other assorted materials, lay propped open aside me, also airing-out in the direct sunshine. Hanging from the lowest branch of a nearby spruce tree, my chest waders (having now been turned inside-out) provided their own slowly dripping cadence, subtly mocking me in their dampened and inanimate state of amusement.

In what normally constitutes one's "famous last words" preceding nearly any calamity, *things had been going just fine.* I'd been slowly working my way up the medium-sized, clearwater creek, fishing the pocket water in search of rainbows. It's a comparatively fast and tumbling stream, with numerous stretches that are choked too tightly by surrounding brush to allow for effective casting. I'd been picking my way along the margins of one such section, where it's necessary to wade upstream along the creek's western bank in order to bypass a particularly thick stand of alders. I had stepped up onto a relatively flat rock that jutted outward from the bank, comfortably stepping off the other side and back into the stream's eight inches of water.

Well . . . that's what was *supposed* to happen, anyway. I'm not sure of what I had *thought* I saw, perhaps misinterpreting a reflection from the morning's low-angle sunlight, but the "eight inches" of water that I had stepped into had somehow turned into a hole some three feet deep, pitching me forward with the unexpected, downward momentum that results in full-fledged belly flop. Ever protective of my fly rod, I had kept it raised and pointed skyward throughout the course of my fall, reminiscent of a biblical staff as I proceeded to part the waters with the authority of Moses himself. (Although, if I remember my catechism correctly, Moses used the power of God—and managed to stay dry in the process—whereas I used the divine power of my face and chest to divide the flowing waters in a somewhat less-than-miraculous fashion.)

So . . . there I sat, patiently waiting for my clothes to dry—at least to a degree where I wouldn't be actively squishing as I waded through the remainder of the day. I continued to marvel at the warmth, stillness, and relatively bug-free status of the morning, conditions that one might be lucky enough to encounter only a few days out of the month on this part of the Peninsula. I took further comfort in the status of my undamaged fly rod, knowing that the day's future had remained out of jeopardy.

As an instinctive and learned reflex, I immediately took advantage of the break in my activity to begin a close inspection of the water's surface in front of me (And yes, I DO realize that such an intensive examination would've proven to be highly beneficial a few moments earlier . . .). Upon doing so, I immediately started to see the telltale signs of emergent insect life, accompanied by some barely discernible surface-rises in the water's few calm pockets.

A hatch was starting to come off, and the trout were already keying into the activity.

While the rise-forms heightened my impatience to get geared up again, I had a far more pressing motivation to re-enter the ranks of the fully clothed angler's club. My best friend and longtime fishing partner, Glen Nielsen, had accompanied me on this sojourn, and had stopped to fish one of the creek's lower riffles as I had hiked ahead. Unless he'd stumbled upon an exceptionally productive stretch of water, he'd likely be working his way around the nearest bend at any moment, discovering me in all my sundrenched and pasty-skinned splendor.

It's been said that the easiest way to tell if you're getting old (or not) is to simply fall down. If people gasp and come running to your aid, you're old. If, instead, they point and laugh hysterically, you can take comfort in the fact that you're still young. Had he seen my epic swan-dive, I have no doubt that Glen would've still viewed me as a very young man indeed. While I had initially been elated that my fall had gone unwitnessed, after sitting on the rock for a while a somewhat odd feeling began to slowly creep in. I was actually surprised to feel a growing pang of regret, knowing just how much Glen would've enjoyed seeing the finer, artistic elements of my recent performance.

Regardless of having missed the actual event, I knew that Glen would receive an almost equal amount of joy in hearing me recount the detailed description of my tumble. One of the most enduring characteristics of our longtime friendship has always been an unguarded sense of honesty, combined with an unflinching embrace of mutual self-deprecation. We had both been somewhat immature and dorky in high school, but unlike many of the other students we possessed a sense of satisfying and realistic self-awareness. We were in no great hurry to "grow up," and we fully embraced the opportunity to act like morons while we could still get away with it. Later in life I would find it quite amusing, if not downright hysterical, to see the shock on some of our former classmate's faces when I had become a police chief in Fairbanks, and Glen had become a highly respected principal and school-district administrator in Anchorage.

As mentioned earlier, I hung with three close friends throughout the duration of high school. Dave Highness was my primary skiing partner; Willy Hall acted as our overall logistics manager, with his parents' house serving as our primary base of operations. Glen completed our foursome, competing most closely with me in striving to provide the group's comic relief. It's kind of funny when I look back on it now, but Glen and I rarely fished together during high school, as summers found us working in separate, remote locations across Alaska. It wouldn't be 'til some years later, once all of the kids from our respective families had grown and gone, that we had more time to connect between Fairbanks and Anchorage, meeting to chase fish across the state.

Regardless of which phase of life I've found myself in, I've always been highly selective when it came to choosing, and spending time with, friends. While I had long since outgrown my previous ranking systems of hierarchy when it came to external categories (such as demonstrated fishing methods or preference of beer) I have fiercely held onto my internal selection criteria for basic friendship. While the former tends to place judgements upon others, I unabashedly defend the latter by embracing the judgement that it squarely places upon myself.

Like most people, I suppose, I tend to place casual acquaintances, workmates, and true friends into somewhat separate categories, with

a host of available options and activities deemed acceptable for each. Once again finding appeal in fishing-based analogies, I've come to consider the presence of friends and acquaintances in my life in much the same manner that I view the contents of my considerable number of fly boxes. I have quite a few flies that seem to simply take up space, often appearing to be mostly for show, while others I deem to be highly essential. Some are accessed only rarely—often for highly specific situations—and there are always those few that somehow manage to show up in my collection, with me having no idea where they came from.

The casual acquaintances, fine for short conversations at the store or perhaps running into at large parties, obviously fill the back-of-the-shelf, bottom-tier fly boxes. Many of these flies were store bought or received as gifts, as one doesn't spend the time and energy in learning to tie these seldom-used patterns. There's absolutely nothing *wrong* with these flies, per se, it's simply a matter of fact that you'll rarely spend a lot of time in consideration of their merits, and—when and if you do—you'll likely choose a more favored alternative. One should not get too judgmental or dismissive, however, in their opinion regarding these patterns. A circumstance will occasionally arise where one of these flies may prove to be the only option available, and upon selection will rise to perform in exceedance of expectations (This, by the way, is how a casual acquaintance can sometimes break-through the barrier, ascending into true friendship.)

Workmates have always tended to assume greater prominence in my life, particularly during my career in policing. These relationships take on a higher degree of complexity, due to the camaraderie that develops through the sharing of duties, venting of mutual frustrations, and the greater degree of mutual understanding and respect that results. These are the friends that you'll attend work-related events with and perhaps invite over to your house for smaller gatherings or card games. You'll likely be happy to help with their airport pickups or drop-offs, and—

for those "top tier" work friends—perhaps even help with the dreaded, residential move. (With the number of any staircases involved being directly proportional to the friend's placement within one's tier-structure. . . .)

The flies that best reflect my working friends are what I'd call the "comfortable standards," consisting of my most commonly used streamers and generic, bead-head nymphs. Many of the immediately recognizable dry patterns in my boxes would fit this category as well, to include the standard assortment of Wulffs, gnats, and humpies. The flies picked from these boxes can almost always be counted on to do quite well when picked for the appropriate situation, and you're always glad to have them along and available.

When it comes to friends, though . . . and I mean real, true, friends . . . well, I've never had very many. My three closest friends from school have remained as such, and a couple of guys from my work-life over the years have ascended to this top tier. For me, the litmus test in defining whether someone has the requisite characteristics and capacity to belong in this rarified grouping is really quite simple: *Is this a person that I'd go fishing or hunting with?*

Now, like any hard-and-fast rule, this test likely requires a bit of qualification. When I say "hunting," I don't mean looking for spruce grouse, or hopping in a truck to cruise a back-country road in search of easy game. I'd do that with work friends and wouldn't be *too* overly selective in my screening process, provided the person had a relatively compatible personality, and was willing to bring some snacks. When I talk about a true "hunting friend," I'm speaking about guys like Randy Coffey, who evolved to be my primary moose hunting partner for many years while we worked together at FPD.

Randy and I took a lot of exceptional trips together into some very remote regions of Alaska's backcountry, bringing out a lot of nice moose

in the process. When you and your raft are dropped by floatplane to travel ten days by river through untracked wilderness, you tend to learn a lot about a guy. When you've stashed the motor from your freighter canoe, dragging the boat from a river over to the chain of three lakes that you'll paddle through to reach a moose, you learn even more. And, when a half-ton moose you've shot ends up in the water, and your partner is standing over the depth of his hip-waders as he works to butcher around its ass end . . . well, that's when you learn who your REAL friends are.

Rich Meyer, a City of Fairbanks firefighter that I also got to know quite closely while working at FPD, is another whom I'd place firmly within the "true friends" camp. While we've hunted a few times, we've also taken a lot of exceptional backcountry snowmachine trips together, where attention to detail can potentially mean the difference between life and death—especially at thirty and forty-below. Rich is a lot more mechanically inclined than I am, but he has a way of coaching me through a simple fix on my four-wheeler or snowmachine without making me feel like an idiot. On top of that, he's an excellent poker and cribbage player, both skillsets of which add significant value in my rankings. Rich is just one of those guys who's a lot of fun to hang around with, and one who doesn't feel the need to fill in all periods of silence with unnecessary commentary.

While hunting carries its own parameters, fishing presents an additional level of complexity, and requires some further explanation. If you want to cast some spoons from the ocean shores of Allison Point to pick up some nickel-bright silvers, give me a call! I'll likely be happy to join you, even if we haven't previously spent a ton of time together. If you own a decent boat and want to go bottom-fishing out of Valdez or Seward, I'll relax my stringent screening standards to an even greater degree, happily paying for boat-gas and herring in the process. I'll actually

fish saltwater with just about anyone, provided they're not obnoxious, drunk, or dangerous.

Halibut trips notwithstanding, when I speak of a "true fishing friend," I'm talking about someone who I'd feel comfortable fishing a small trout stream with. These are the guys like Glen, Randy, or Rich, and they don't come along often in one's life. These are the "go-to" flies in my box. These are the elk-hair caddis, parachute Adams, and black foam ant that I'll take as my only three flies for a day spent on my home water. These are the patterns that have repeatedly performed and delivered for me in the past, giving me the trust and confidence to choose them as my first picks for primary exploration, even when entering new and unfamiliar waters. They're called "go-to" for a reason.

It can be a bit odd to talk about friends in the context of fly fishing, as the majority of my time spent on creeks and rivers is spent fishing in solitude. Even when fishing with a close friend like Glen, we're split-up through the greater portions of the day as we leapfrog our way up or down a chosen stream. We'll only come together occasionally, most often to compare notes on which patterns are currently working best, before separating again. (I particularly enjoy making a casual, offhand comment as I walk off, addressing some minor peculiarity that I'd noticed in his casting or drift technique, as he'll later accuse me of trying to "get inside his head . . .")

I've long debated with myself in pondering a final, friendship-related question: When I have an opportunity to fish a great stream, is it better to fish with a friend, or fish by myself? I know that some of my most joyous days this past year were spent fishing rivers and creeks with Glen on the Kenai Peninsula, out in Katmai, and even down in Argentina. However, some of the most powerful and introspective emotions that I experienced during this same year occurred while fishing my solitary grayling waters in the Interior's highlands. I've come to the

conclusion that there's likely no set answer, as any particular day, week, or set of circumstances may dictate what's best for the moment. I know myself well enough to realize that I need periods of occasional solitude, as I've found that conditions that allow for true, contemplative thought are somewhat rare, and shouldn't be taken for granted.

Conversely, the opportunities to maintain close friendships through fishing should be cherished as well. The day following my epic bellyflop into that small, Peninsula creek, Glen and I were once again fishing together—this time on another, slightly larger stream that's a few miles closer to his cabin in Sterling. The particular creek we were fishing receives its run of sockeye a few weeks earlier than the first one; numerous salmon were already present, and we were targeting the rainbows and dollies that shadowed them. We were fishing one of the stream's upper-most segments, wading back and forth through its tumbling sections to fish the calm, in-between spots where the sockeye would tend to hold. Frustrated with having hung-up on a branch along a particularly tight stretch, I had to spend a few minutes undoing a tangle as Glen continued to work his way downstream.

Having finally untangled and re-rigged, I started working my way down the creek to catch up with Glen. Coming around a bend, ever cautious for the potential to meet a brown bear along the salmon-filled waters, I was keeping my eyes focused ten to twenty yards downstream. Through the screening cover of encroaching alders, a flash of white suddenly caught my eye. It was, of course, Glen . . . standing in his underwear. He stood dripping on the streambank, struggling mightily as he attempted to pull his waterlogged turtleneck up and over his head. His pack had been thrown down beside him, and his inside-out waders were already hung from a tree, allowing for proper drainage.

Sometimes it's worthwhile to fish with a friend. ☉

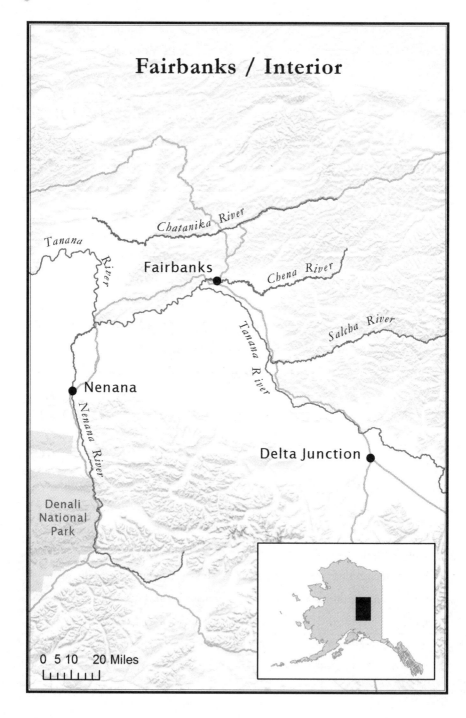

Fairbanks / Interior

Tanana

Chatanika River

Tanana

River

Fairbanks

Chena River

Tanana River

Salcha River

Nenana

Nenana River

Delta Junction

Denali
National
Park

0 5 10   20 Miles

Chapter Ten

SPECIAL PLACES #1:
My Grayling Home Water

If you can't be with the one you love,
love the one you're with.
—**Stephen Stills,** *Love the One You're With;* 1970 Self-Titled Album

I f I was forced to fish *one stream only* for the rest of my days, with
the choice being made irrespective of logistical or financial con-
straints, I'd likely pick one of two rivers in the Katmai region of Bristol
Bay. I've grown quite fond of these particular drainages, as the size, power,
and unbridled tenacity of their resident rainbows is without equal,
providing a rather heady incentive for future returns.

Life, however, rarely achieves complete perfection. And while the
streams and rivers of Katmai are always whispering their soft, siren's
song within the background of my consciousness, the remoteness of
these rivers makes such a dream prohibitive. While I'll save my funds
to travel there occasionally, it's simply not realistic for me to assume
I'll enjoy those waters for more than a few, treasured journeys over the
course of the next several years. Like it or not, I'm a realist—and I'm not
holding my breath in anticipation for a genie to magically appear from
my fly box and grant such a wish.

I'm fully aware, however, of the fact that I am already *far* luckier
than many of the fishermen I know. I live less than an hour's drive away

from one of the most pristinely beautiful rivers to be found north of the Alaska range, and over the years it has grown to fulfill the lion's share of my fly-fishing requirements. A true blue-ribbon fishery, its upper reaches provide me with countless, wadable stretches that I can easily hike into, providing for a day's excursion that represents the most minimal of preparatory efforts. It's extraordinarily easy for me to simply grab my gear and go—often at a moment's notice—without having to spend the time and worry associated with extensive travel. (Not to mention boat haulage, ramp fees, and car ferrying.) I've noted that, as I have gotten older, inertia seems to present as much of a threat to me as anything else; any removal of potential obstructions that allows for me to fish quickly, easily, and more often is now considered a superior alternative.

I often speak in terms of the perfect trout stream, and this one is it. Easily wadable with a gravelly, freestone bottom, its waters can run remarkably clear through the Interior's hot, summer months. The variable, topographic pitch found amongst its upper forks provides for intermittent sections of exceptional holding water, and its broad, bordering gravel bars provide for a snag-free, fly caster's dream. This perfect "trout stream," however, requires me to address one glaring contradiction: There is not a single trout to be found there. The river boasts a small population of whitefish, and while I've never actively fished for them, I'll occasionally pick one up when fishing very small nymphs. For my primary angling purposes, however, this water is ruled by a fish that offers—at least in certain respects—a superior substitute for the larger rainbows found to the south: The arctic grayling.

One could certainly argue that grayling deserve their placement among the defined boundaries of a "trout stream;" as a fellow member of the *Salmonidae* family, they are closely related to trout, char, and whitefish. Over the course of the spring and early summer, the largest of these sail-finned beauties will consistently move to the uppermost reaches of the drainage, far from the populated campgrounds that dominate the river's lower stretches. This seasonal, migratory characteristic provides me with the degree of separation that I require for my frequent, solitary outings, and it's quite rare for me to encounter another fisherman on the stretches that I regularly hike into. It's primarily for this reason that I can't bring myself to disclose this drainage by its specific name, though my pathetic attempts at secrecy can likely be overcome by all but the densest of readers through the simplest of map searches and accompanying clues.

Planning my standard day's sojourn, I can feel myself once again falling slave to my father's deeply ingrained influences. Having grown up to frequently associate a brief, food-related experience as a component of any successful outing, I'll plan on leaving the house early enough to allow for a quick stop at *Larae's* bake shop, where I can drink a cup of coffee and munch on one of their maple-bacon cinnamon rolls while briefly perusing the morning's *Daily News-Miner.* I don't feel too guilty about the extra calories, as I'll be doing plenty of hiking and wading throughout the day. Having fulfilled the duties and obligations of this genetic imperative, I'll head onward in search of one of my preferred roadway pull-offs, likely choosing the first that presents my one, required condition: Having zero vehicles present.

Once parked off the roadway, I'll grab my gear and hike towards the river as quickly as I can. If I hear a car approaching, I'll laughably crouch behind the bed of my pickup, or do my best ninja-leap into the brush, as I don't want to visibly tout the fact that I'm stopped at a prime departure spot for fishing. (This is also the reason I eschew exterior mounted rod holders and trout-related decals on my truck, as I'd prefer that its presence—regardless of location—doesn't loudly proclaim: "Anglers be here!") Doping-up to the minimum extent possible in the ever-present battle against mosquitos, I'll begin my planned route for the day.

If this is my first trek of the season into any particular section, I'll need to set any preconceived notions and expectations aside. The high waters of early spring will routinely deposit and remove logjams with surprising ease, and the well-defined channels of the previous season can be found to be unrecognizable upon return. This component of yearly mystery adds to the stream's appeal, however, as there are always new puzzles to find and solve. It seems that whenever I start to bemoan the loss of a particularly favorite hole, a newly created stretch of favorable holding water will inevitably be found by day's end. I'll plan on hitting the river at the lowermost point of my forecast route, fishing my way upward until the time—or the level of accumulating, afternoon thunder-clouds—dictates that I turn around. At that point I'll likely change-up flies from the patterns proven to be optimal thus far, conducting a greater degree of experimentation as I work my way back downriver.

Grayling seem to inevitably prefer their offerings when presented on the surface; a characteristic the places me forever in their debt, and one which I'm more than happy to oblige. Whether I'm fishing standard dries, foam terrestrials, or small deer-hair shrews, watching the decep-tively casual progression of a grayling's rise—from their initial, seemingly casual lift-off to the final, fiercely focused take—never gets old. Most of the rainbows, brookies, and browns that I've fished for elsewhere seem to retreat in spooky shyness when their midday haunts reach a certain degree of illumination; it's just the opposite here. Grayling love to lie in wait while sunlight bathes the water's surface, and such dauntingly bright conditions seem to ring an irrepressible dinner bell for the start of their daily hunts. Such affinity for midday feeding provides an addi-tional bonus for me, as it precludes the need for an exceptionally early start. (The requirement of which would constitute a gross departure from what I'd otherwise deem to be an acceptable morning.)

As I alluded to in the previous chapter, there are three "go-to" flies that constitute 90 percent or more of my use while fishing this river. One was determined largely by accident, though I'll take full credit for its discovery, as it was the direct result of my conscious decision to stop and wait, pausing to thoroughly scan and evaluate current conditions, before simply jumping into my fishing. The particular day of this discovery occurred nearly thirty years ago, but I still remember it as if it were yesterday.

I was walking up onto a particularly nice, looping bend in the river—a stretch that has remained as one of my favorites to this day. I had noticed a few medium-sized caddis flies fluttering in the sunshine as I got close to the water, and I was prepared to tie on an appropriate imitation and immediately get started. However, not knowing if the flies were fresh, or remnants from an earlier hatch, I decided to sit on the edge of a large spruce snag that was conveniently positioned for surveillance, spending a few moments in close observance of the water's edge.

I had sat on the snag for all of ten seconds, intently scanning the surface of the water, when an inordinately loud and buggy-sounding "splat" found the back of my bare neck, causing my immediate (and decidedly less than masculine) swatting response. Pulling my hand away, the half-crushed remnant of a large, winged carpenter ant fell to my thigh. Within the space of a minute I'd swatted two or three more, and upon further inspection towards the base of the spruce log I could see that hundreds of ants were crawling about.

I now refocused my observational efforts towards the numerous spruce trunks and downed sweepers that bordered this stretch of river, and it wasn't long before I realized just how many ants seemed to be populating the trees. Up until that point I'd never placed ant patterns among my serious contenders for the drainage; I had a few

Chernobyl-type flies in the terrestrial portion of my box, left over from a prior trip to Colorado, and I took one out and trimmed its body down to an appropriate size with my clippers. Deftly flicking it to an extended slow-water slick, immediately downstream from a half-submerged sweeper, the poor Jenny Craig ant never stood a chance. Quickly taken by one of the largest fish I'd hooked all week, the day evolved into a virtual "ant-o-rama," requiring me to trim-down my two remaining specimens before all three eventually disintegrated from overuse.

I returned home that evening, quickly retiring to my tying bench to craft a batch of custom, black foam beauties, each with a bit of crystal-flash for the wing, and a small, front-of-thorax post of vertical, white foam for enhanced visibility. If the weather is hot, particularly during good ant years, this is the only fly necessary to catch fish continuously along many of the spruce-bordered stretches of river.

While my ant pattern may represent the silver-standard for the drainage, the elk-hair caddis deserves to retain its spot atop the gold medal podium. My primary prospecting fly, its visibility, floatability, and effectiveness at matching the preponderance of surface life on the river is second to none. It's hard for me to even begin to estimate how many fish I've hooked from the drainage's upper forks with this pattern, as its certainly within the thousands by now. Hiking upstream on a warm, sunny, and low-water afternoon, a size-fourteen elk-hair caddis—when cast appropriately above a holding fish and allowed to float down in natural, drag-free drift—apparently presents a morsel for consideration that has no equal in the grayling's universe.

I try not to get too gluttonous in my appetites on any particular stretch of water, as I like to rest the fish when possible, and not catch every single one within a given hole. However, when coming back downstream and fishing stretches that I'd previously fished up through, (or, on those rare occasions when fish have promptly risen to inspect my caddis but rejected it as somehow suspect) I'll switch to a gray parachute Adams as my secondary prospector. The Adams, like the caddis, provides the requisite visibility for my inevitably aging eyesight, and it always seems to present the properly buggy profile necessary to push a reluctant grayling beyond its point of hesitation.

Yes, I could fish my home water through nearly the entirety of summer using only three patterns, a fact whose disclosure to certain friends may prove ruinous to my feigned status as some kind of dry-fly savant. There are certainly circumstances that occasionally allow for other patterns and experimentation; we had a decent hatch of small grasshoppers occur a few summers ago, and small foam hoppers worked quite nicely through its duration. I continue to explore different nymphing methods whenever there's a pause in dry activity, and I caught my first grayling on a San Juan worm this past fall while messing around with various dry-dropper combinations. I find the dusky portion of evening to be the best time to fish small, deer-hair shrew patterns, though I'm sure this is far more reflective of the shrew's peak time of activity, rather than that of the grayling.

As the summer season slowly progresses, I'll keep my fingers crossed for continuous hot, sunny weather. The quality of fishing in the drainage's upper forks varies in inverse proportion to the overall water level; the lower the water gets, the better the fishing. Periods of extreme low water force the grayling into concentrated holding stretches, and into the tight margins along the stream's banks. Sight fishing becomes easier and easier, and I've had days where—whenever I spotted a specific fish—I could virtually guarantee that it'd end up in my net.

While I purposely resist many applications of modern technology, I've found the stream-level data that's transmitted from a NOAA measuring station in the river's mid-reaches and posted to their website in real time to be invaluable. Isolated, heavy showers in the surrounding hills can change stream-flows in the upper forks considerably, and it's nice to be able to check this data from home when deciding if a day's trip would be worthwhile. Flows below 16.5 feet will allow for adequate stream crossings at my favorite points, and sub-16 measurements mean a day of carefree, easy wading. When levels fall to 15.5 feet and below, you'll likely have to wrestle me to the ground to keep me home on a sunny day. Mow the lawn?! I'm pretty sure that's why God invented Astroturf . . .

Moving into fall, fishing the clear and rapidly cooling waters once again mentally transports me to the autumnal fishing of my youth. The grayling are no longer scattered freely throughout the drainage; the larger fish will have started to back down into the river's mid-reaches, tending to congregate along the deeper stretches as the margins start to freeze. I'll spend mornings and early afternoons uncharacteristically fishing a variety of subsurface patterns, with dries reserved for an occasional flurry of late-afternoon activity. The advance of the season will eventually present a close race to the finish, where my final trip of the year will either be cut short by excessive icing in my rod's guides, or upon my discovery that the grayling are finally gone, having backed all the way down into the deep, over-wintering channels of the featureless lower river, where I really have no desire to fish.

In addition to granting me many season's worth of exercise, enjoyment, and personal mental-health therapy, my favorite home drainage has also provided for the introduction and continuing education for a new generation of fly fishermen in our family. I've been proud to watch both our daughter Courtney and son Casey learn to fly cast on the river's upper reaches, excitedly bringing in their own grayling for an appreciative inspection and release. My brother Dave was able to bring my nephews Ville and Veikko over from Finland to catch their first Alaskan grayling with me, and I was particularly overjoyed on another

December Dawn: The City of Fairbanks lies shrouded under a layer of ice-fog, as an 11:00 a.m. sunrise illuminates the peaks of the Alaska Range mountains. PHOTO BY DAN HOFFMAN

Billy and Bernard Hoffman - Lake Fork of the Gunnison
1943

Dan and Bill Hoffman - Lake Fork of the Gunnison
2015

Fathers & Sons: Author's father and grandfather above; author and father below. PHOTOS FROM THE HOFFMAN FAMILY COLLECTION

In the Genes: My great grandfather, William Hagerman, fly fishing in Southwest Colorado. Painting by noted western landscape artist Helen Brooks Hagerman, circa 1930. FROM THE HOFFMAN FAMILY COLLECTION

Brothers Fishing: Author (right) with older brother David at Sylvan Lake, Colorado. PHOTO FROM THE HOFFMAN FAMILY COLLECTION

Us Kids: Author (rear middle) with brother David and sisters Diane and Donna in Lake City, Colorado. PHOTO FROM THE HOFFMAN FAMILY COLLECTION

High School Years: The author fishing for early spring grayling on the waters of upper Montana Creek in the Susitna River valley.

PHOTO FROM THE HOFFMAN FAMILY COLLECTION

Guiding Days: The author has precious few photos from his mid-80s guiding days in Katmai; prior to cell phones, nearly all pictures were taken of clients using their own cameras. PHOTOS FROM THE HOFFMAN FAMILY COLLECTION

The Big Game: Author with a football-shaped American Creek rainbow.
PHOTO BY GLEN NIELSEN

Dad & Mom: Author with his father Bill (above) on the banks of the Kulik River in Alaska. Author with his mother Phyllis (below) on the Gunnison's Lake Fork in Colorado. PHOTOS FROM THE HOFFMAN FAMILY COLLECTION

Catching a Trout with a Bunny: Swinging a bunny leech from the mouth of the Kulik River into Nonvianuk Lake is a good way to find some nice lake trout.

PHOTO SEQUENCE BY CHUCK BABBITT

Fall Beauty: Autumn in the highlands of Interior Alaska makes for a stunning grayling fishery.

Arctic Grayling Beauty: The author on his home water with a nice arctic grayling (above). The gorgeous colors of the grayling's dorsal fin shine in the sun.

PHOTOS BY DAN HOFFMAN

Rainbow: The author fishes for rainbows on the Upper Russian River.

PHOTO BY GLEN NIELSEN

By Water: Our chariot awaits on the Kenai River.

PHOTO BY DAN HOFFMAN

Double Rainbow: Author (left) and Glen Nielsen enjoy a Katmai double rainbow. PHOTO BY DAN HOFFMAN

By Air: A Katmai Air DeHavilland Beaver greets the sunrise at the mouth of the Kulik River. PHOTO BY DAN HOFFMAN

Fishing Pals: Author and his primary fishing partner, Glen Nielsen, on the Kenai.

PHOTO BY DAN HOFFMAN

Keeping Cool: Gwen Hoffman keeps her cool on the banks of American Creek

PHOTO BY DAN HOFFMAN

A Beauty: Glen Nielsen with a beautiful Kulik River rainbow.

PHOTO BY DAN HOFFMAN

True Happiness: Author with a 12 lb. American Creek rainbow.

PHOTO BY GLEN NIELSEN

Giving Back: An arctic grayling on the author's home water
is brought in for release.

PHOTO BY DAN HOFFMAN

occasion to have Ville accompanied by his grandfather—my dad—for a great day of dry-fly fishing on the river.

Yes, it isn't Katmai . . . but in this world, there isn't much that is. I wasn't quite sure what to expect when I decided to settle in Fairbanks after college, and the first impressions I carried of my home river may have been colored with a small amount of condescension as I continued to revel in my recent recollections from Bristol Bay. However, I suppose my ultimate experience might share some similarities with someone who has had to navigate an "arranged marriage."

I would assume that—in at least some of those cases of orchestrated betrothal, a period of initial unfamiliarity and apprehension slowly morphs into one of continuous discovery, where appreciation for all the "little things" steadily grows, ultimately culminating in the sense of true happiness that results through a lifetime of sustained evolution and commitment. Upon reflection, I'd say that such an analogy perfectly sums up my relationship with the home waters that I frequent. While I may not have started out by "being with the one I loved," I can now truly say that I love the one I'm with. ⊙

Chapter Eleven

THE CURSE OF GAINFUL
EMPLOYMENT,
and the Work of Stripping Streamers

"Streep! Streep! Streeeeeeeeeep!" The heavily-accented words had repeated incessantly in my head all evening, elbowing their way to the forefront of my consciousness. I burrowed down further into my sleeping bag, seeking a means of potential escape from my brain's looping recollection. Perhaps I just needed to take a deep breath, slowly exhale, and close my eyes in relaxation as I prepared for a comfortable night's sleep upon the sandbar where we'd pitched our camp . . .

"Streeeeeeeeep!!!"

I had to chuckle to myself; I was a *long* way from home, having escaped Fairbanks' midwinter doldrums in search of an angling escape. Gwen and I had made the two-day journey of connecting flights from Fairbanks to the town of San Carlos de Bariloche in southern Argentina, connecting with my fishing partner Glen and his wife Patti in Buenos Aires along the way. A stunningly beautiful, Bavarian-looking town, Bariloche is nestled in the mountains along the shores of Lake Nahuel Huapi, with the Patagonian region boasting several prominent trout-fishing rivers in its immediate vicinity.

Glen and I had fished the Manso on our first day, a beautiful river that drains to the far side of the Andes, the only Pacific Ocean drainage we'd see on this trip. All four of us floated the nearby Limay the following day, catching some beautiful fish and thoroughly enjoying our outfitter's extensive, lunch-time cookout on the banks of the beautiful river. For the next part of the trip, Glen and I had left our wives in town to guard the local supply of red wine, while we spent two days and nights floating the Collón Cura river, some 175 kilometers to the north.

We were fishing for browns and rainbows, and the river had not disappointed. We'd both caught our fair share of each, switching-off for the prime, front-seat position in the raft at the halfway point of each day. Though we'd fought the rise of some pretty steady winds in the afternoon hours, it didn't affect our casting too much, as we were slinging heavy streamers on sink-tip lines. Amidst the cadence of our repeated casting, our joyous and irrepressible Argentinian guide—Facundo— could not help himself from providing his primary means of coaching and encouragement, helpfully reminding us after nearly every cast that we needed to quickly strip our flies inward in a punctual, jerking retrieval.

"Streeep! Streeep! Streeeeeeeep!!!!"

Such repetitions notwithstanding, we were thoroughly enjoying the trip, feeling unbelievably spoiled as we floated into the first night's camp. Our outfitter's support crew had already arrived to set things up and were in the process of cooking dinner. After shucking our waders and changing into some sweatpants, we wandered over to find a separate and fully stocked bar tent, an amenity that I could definitely see myself getting used to. Sipping on a small tumbler of whisky as I sat by the crackling campfire, (and still working to exorcise Facundo's looping recitations from my mind . . .) I had started to become vaguely aware of another, developing issue. For the first time in my fishing life, the repeated casting and stripping of streamers in strong winds had started to aggravate my right elbow—to a point where I was worried about how it might fare the following day.

While some rest and ibuprofen solved most of the immediate problem, the elbow would continue to be an issue throughout much of my upcoming fishing year. It posed no major challenges when fishing the summer's Interior grayling, but the autumn rainbows of Katmai necessitated my switch to a right-handed reel, allowing me to pass the rod over to my left when actually fighting those incredibly strong fish.

I'd chucked and stripped a lot of heavy streamers back in my guiding days, but it's not something that I often do now. The majority of my efforts in fly fishing (as are most of my efforts in life) are more quiescent in nature, targeting the achievement of a drag-free drift.

Whether fishing dry flies, nymphs, or egg patterns, I'm normally seeking to mimic my offering's natural counterparts in the water, all of whom tend to float along at a pace coinciding with the stream's natural current. If one allows a belly to form in their fly line, drawn downstream by the water's faster mid-currents, the following fly will eventually be pulled forward at a speed greater than that of the surrounding water, instantly raising the suspicions of any feeding fish. Food floats to them naturally, and it does so at the pace of the current.

Similarly, if one fails to position and mend their line accordingly in such a manner to allow for an unobstructed drift, the line may end up causing drag, exerting a degree of upstream pull upon the fly that causes it to drift too slowly in relation to the current. This will cause the same alarm bells to ring within the instinctive centers of the fish's brain, as they instantly perceive something to be a little "off" as the prospective morsel comes drifting along in an unnatural—and therefore disconcerting—manner.

When fishing streamers, pursuit of such a drag-free presentation is rarely a consideration.

While one might occasionally float a streamer in a dead-drift style, particularly in very cold waters where fish might be sluggish and less prone to chase darting prey, it's important to remember what you're trying to imitate, and how your fly's natural counterpart normally acts in the water. I should place "fly" in quotations, as streamer patterns are not meant to mimic any type of insect whatsoever. These are primarily baitfish patterns, most often tied to resemble a swimming sculpin, minnow, or leach. As such, they are designed—and most often intended—to be fished with varying degrees of motion, imitating the movements of their natural doppelgangers as they dart about and swim through the currents.

In some respects, this makes fishing the streamer much easier, as one doesn't need to make the number of mends and micro-adjustments to the line necessary to achieve or maintain a dead drift. The streamer is often purposefully stripped across the current in darting, jerking motions, with bone-jarring strikes often occurring during the halting, mid-strip pauses.

Similarly, the fly can be allowed to drift down and across the current in a slowing, arcing manner, purposefully allowing for the drag in one's line to cause the requisite swing at the end of the drift. Fish seem to instinctively line up for the end-point of such swings, to which any streamer aficionado can attest. However, make no mistake about it: Casting and stripping streamers all day—especially in the winds of the Collón Cura, was the closest thing to "work" I'd experienced as a fly caster in quite a while.

The epic adventure that we'd taken to Argentina in February was more than just a midwinter escape, it was somewhat of a retirement present that I'd promised to myself. Having left my final job just two weeks prior, I'd had a few opportunities at home (and during some of our marathon airplane flights) to reflect on my forty-year work history. I'd had a hell of great run—all of it within Alaska—and I was now looking forward to abandoning the more restrictive components of life that normally accompany one's gainful employment.

I had only one, true "shit job" during the entire course of my working life. After finishing my freshman year of high school, I'd signed-on to be a dishwasher at the Alyeska Hotel in Girdwood, where my Dad was the manager. While the ski resort was obviously closed for the summer, a steady stream of Princess Cruise tourists kept the hotel's kitchen busy, as Alyeska was a scheduled lunch stop for their buses on the way to visit the Portage Glacier. I spoke awhile back about the power of smell to invoke memories; to this day, the smell of thousand-island salad dressing and cigarette ashes immediately takes me back to that cramped and steamy scullery. (Reflecting the putrid and singularly nasty habit of elderly tourists who commonly used their half-done salad plates as an ashtray . . .)

I was tempted to quit more than a few times, but when you have to come home and see your manager sitting across the dinner table—the same guy you're hoping to borrow the car keys from later that night—well, let's just say I figured I'd better stick it out and satisfy my summer job commitment. Looking back now, though, I'm glad I took the job, as it taught me an invaluable lesson at a relatively early age: A future in the sanitary kitchen arts was not one that I wanted to work towards.

I've always regarded myself as a rather forward-looking person, even at a relatively young age, and I directly credit my upbringing and tutelage as a stream fisherman as a major factor in achieving this orientation. When one looks to fish in any type of moving water, there are many factors that must be immediately considered and planned for. What kind of fish might be there? Where will they be holding? What are they likely eating? If I can produce an acceptable substitute, is there a way I can float it into the right spot without spooking them? If I hook a decent fish, where can I land it? The questions and consideration of variables can go on and on; the fisherman always needs to be looking well beyond his own location in the water, often times several yards up or downstream, in order to anticipate conditions and plan for the best course of action.

As a result of these forward-leaning characteristics, and in consideration of my recent determination that automatic dishwashers were likely invented for a reason, I began to earnestly search for alternatives that might be available for my next summer's employment.

This search led to my application for (and acceptance into) Alaska's Youth Conservation Corps program, resulting in three summers of outstanding field work that I've previously described.

A connection through my YCC work led to summer employment in Katmai—first at Brooks Lodge, and then ultimately at Kulik. In between and after these other jobs, I also spent summers working for the Alaska Department of Fish and Game on a remote study of the proposed Susitna River hydroelectric dam, high in the upper reaches of the Talkeetna Mountains, as well as spending a summer on the far western coast of Alaska, banding waterfowl for the U.S. Fish and Wildlife service. The summers of high school and college provided some wonderful experiences, and I'd often thought I would do these jobs for free if they'd just let me keep working. As my college years neared their close, however, I had to start thinking in more practical terms.

My seasonal jobs had been great, but most didn't seem to lead to solid, year-round prospects. I was also reaching a difficult point of realization and indecision when it came to my chosen field. While I'd done quite well in my studies of wildlife biology, it seemed that all the really great jobs were being done by seasonal field technicians, as I'd already been doing. When I took a good look at the relatively few p full-time biologists that I knew, it appeared they spent the majority of their time compiling data gathered by others, crafting computerized population models in their offices, and writing to publish papers in pertinent scientific journals.

Doing computer work in an office wasn't quite what I'd been shooting for; I was looking for employment that offered a bit of excitement, while providing for a higher sense of purpose as well. I hungered for stability, but also sought a definitive timeline—one where I could get in, work my ass off, and then get out at an early enough age to enjoy the rest of my life. If I was going to position myself for an optimal path of "drag-free drift," it was time to throw a significant mend into my line.

After wrapping up my degree and spending my last summer and fall guiding at Kulik, I headed to the small town of Sitka on the Southeast Panhandle, where I'd been accepted to attend the Alaska Department of Public Safety's police training academy. At the time it was still run under a fairly intense, boot-camp model of contrived stress and sleep deprivation, a style that's been relaxed somewhat in recent years. I learned many of the primary ins-and-outs to being a cop and enjoyed the mix of classmates from various municipal police departments and state agencies across the state of Alaska.

Law enforcement work was a real eye-opener for me; while I had not considered myself to have had a necessarily sheltered upbringing, in retrospect it had indeed been pretty insular. It didn't take me long to realize just how many people truly crazy people are out there running around in this world, barely functioning in our midst. The average citizen believes that adequate, societal "safety nets" must *surely* be in place for these people; in actuality, the resources and capacity for such programs rarely exists, and many commonly fall through the cracks.

Spending a full career working in Alaskan law enforcement, I saw the very best that our state has to offer—as well as the very worst. While I hate to burst the bubble of all the Discovery Channel idealists out there, Alaska is not a completely unspoiled paradise when it comes to the human condition. Many of the military members, university students, and industrial-camp workers who move here find themselves isolated from the support networks of family and friends. Residents from outlying villages who move into the cities struggle with these same issues, often exacerbated by factors of cultural displacement. Add in the ingredients of bone- chilling cold and extended winter darkness, and you might start to understand why our state tops the charts in per capita rates of alcoholism, depression, suicide, and violent crime. Now toss in the number of "end-of-the-roaders" from the Lower 48 who inevitably make their way here, woefully unprepared in seeking their piece of paradise, (and where there'll *surely* be no police—or government of any kind—to bother them . . .) and you have a population that presents more than its share of policing challenges.

In fly-fishing terms, police work rarely allows for one to simply "go with the flow," making small mends while one waits in relaxed fashion to see what evolves. This is the hard work of stripping streamers, where directed and purposeful actions are often necessary to achieve a desirable outcome. While I'd be the first to argue that the current state of policing in America requires intensive scrutiny, with some areas begging for constructive reform, many who attempt to shape the narrative on these issues are woefully ignorant of the realities involved. Just as the jerking, directed retrieval of a heavy streamer might shock the peaceful sensibilities of the chalk- stream fishing, dry-fly purist, so can the immediate establishment of authority and containment by police be perceived as "heavy-handed," especially by those who've never had to deal with the consequences of failure.

Sticking with fishing analogies, I suppose I could offer one additional observation from my career in policing. As a small child being raised to fish, I'd been taught in the mode of our time and location, where stocked streams encouraged one to try and "catch their limit" whenever possible. A successful outing was measured by a full creel, and the thought of releasing a nice-sized fish back into the water was almost unheard of. Fast forwarding several decades, I cannot even remember the last time that I killed a trout. Even the most remote drainages in Southwest Alaska are routinely visited by the over 100 fly-out lodges operating in the region, and the populations of wild trout that inhabit those pristine waters would be decimated in short order if anglers started keeping any portion of their catches.

Luckily, in terms of job security for those still working in policing, our criminal justice system appears to have adopted this same, enlightened ethos. While the incredibly resourceful and perennially short-staffed trooper posts and police departments across the state continue to do an admirable job in finding and arresting those who threaten the safety of our society, our courts have seemingly decided to embrace a "catch-and-release" model as well, thereby ensuring a never ending, renewable supply of offenders.

I now have the luxury of being able to look back on a significant portion of my life, and I feel incredibly fortunate for the opportunities that presented themselves. Challenges and minor complaints aside, I loved my career in policing—it allowed me to serve an amazing community, working in partnership with some of the finest individuals I've ever known. I've often wondered if I would've been happier if I'd stuck with outdoor-related field work, even if it had meant giving up much of the security and benefits that I've attained. I guess I'll never know, but I'm not going to lose any sleep over it. I *do* know that I wouldn't have met my wife if I'd followed a different course; that reason alone is more than enough for me to be satisfied with my decisions.

Initially, it would've been easier for me to maintain the path of drift I'd set through college, but at some point I realized that it often takes a higher degree of energy and effort to achieve one's desired, long-term result. It takes *hard work* to get things done, and when big trout are being pursued, the comparatively strenuous exercise of repeatedly casting heavy, sink-tip lines, followed by the continuous effort of stripping streamers, may be required in order to achieve success. It'll likely prove to be no less enjoyable, as evidenced through my recent Argentinian experience, but make no mistake—it's work. ◉

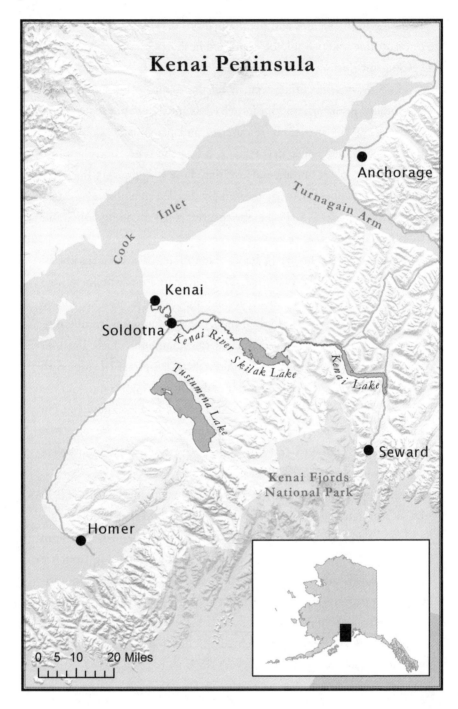

Kenai Peninsula

● Anchorage

Turnagain Arm

Cook Inlet

Kenai ●

Soldotna ●

Kenai River

Skilak Lake

Kenai Lake

Tustumena Lake

● Seward

Kenai Fjords
National Park

Homer ●

0 5 10   20 Miles

Chapter Twelve

SPECIAL PLACES #2:
The Kenai Peninsula

Within the cheerleading circles of our state's tourism boards and promotional organizations, the Kenai Peninsula is often referred to as "Alaska's playground." It's easy to see why, as there's an incredibly diverse range of opportunities awaiting the adventurous traveler, all packed within the relatively close confines (by Alaskan standards, anyway . . .) of this 24,000-square-mile expanse of magnificent, jaw-dropping beauty.

Throughout much of Alaska, barriers to access resulting from our roadless surroundings lead to many regions maintaining a state of perennial isolation. Further prohibited by the high cost of bush air-travel, and with a lack of any support infrastructure at many prospective locations, most longtime Alaskan residents will never get to see some of the most incredible areas within our state. This is not the case with the Kenai Peninsula.

A journey of only two hours by car from the metropolis of Anchorage will lead southward around the shores of Turnagain arm, where one's neck quickly tires from the back-and-forth, tennis fan's motion that results from scanning opposite sides of the highway for Dall sheep and beluga whales. Bypassing Indian, Girdwood, and Portage, then turning sharply to bisect the towering mountains of Turnagain pass, one drops down the far side of the divide to arrive at Tern Lake Junction, known simply as the "Y" by most Alaskan residents. Head left and you'll stay on Alaska's Seward Highway for 36 more miles, proceeding through Moose Pass and ending in the coastal port of Seward. A turn to the right provides one's initiation to the Sterling Highway, with the roadway reaching its terminus at the town of Homer, some 140 miles distant.

Homer and its seaside spit are exceptionally beautiful, and Seward offers some first-rate saltwater fishing opportunities. But, as far as my own flyfishing explorations go, the playground that's spread before me presents a slightly more restricted profile. The portion of the Peninsula where I'll spend the majority of my time is more centrally located, and is anchored by its namesake river, the Kenai. With its name reflecting the shortened version of its historic regional inhabitants—the Kenaitze Tribe of Indians, the Athabascan peoples of the Kahtnuht'ana Dena'ina were the first to marvel at the bounties supplied by the river's mesmerizing, jadelike waters.

The flowing colors of the Kenai are indeed quite striking and markedly different from those of any other drainage that I fish throughout the state. All of Alaska's rivers and streams can be plotted on a gradient of appearance and transparency, encompassing a wide range of conditions. Crystalline drainages in the Interior uplands will drop into the tannin-stained waters of the flats, and the gray, milky flows of glacial streams will often mix with the muddier, silt-laden portions of their chocolaty, lower drainages. One will not be able to see a sockeye dipped from the Copper River until their net is lifted completely from the water, as many of Alaska's silt-laden waters hold their secrets quite close.

The Kenai River, in a class all of its own, presents a rather unique profile as a result of its geography. Kenai lake, the source of the river's origin, collects the bulk of its waters from a host of surrounding, melting glaciers. The body of water is very large, however, providing the volume and time necessary to allow for its heavier glacial sediments to settle. The remaining, suspended silt—ultra fine in nature—flows outward from the lake in a wondrously perfect proportion- not enough to significantly diminish the water's short-distance clarity, but with just enough refractive capacity to lend a striking, bluish-green tinge to the water. The river will flow south for approximately 17 miles, where it will empty into its intermediate reservoir of Skilak Lake. There, an additional amount of surrounding glacial runoff will add to the payload of suspended silt, with an accompanying degree of settling occurring as well. Resuming its journey at the outlet, the turquoise waters of the Kenai will continue their flow southwards for another 57 miles, eventually slowing to a series of looping, tidally influenced meanders before empty into the waters of Cook Inlet.

The great thing about the region is that it offers so many possibilities. When I drive down to fish the Peninsula, I'll normally base my explorations out of the small community of Sterling. My fishing partner Glen was wise enough to purchase a small cabin there several years ago, and he's gracious enough to allow for its use—whether he's around or not. There's not a lot to be found in Sterling itself; it's pretty much a wide spot in the road, with a gas station providing the area's finest cuisine. No matter, though—the St. Elias brewpub is a mere 15 miles further south in the tourist's mecca of Soldotna, and they make a pretty killer pizza. Far more importantly, however, are the nearly dozen rivers and smaller streams that lie within an hour's radius of the cabin.

When picking the target of my day's activities on the Peninsula, my first decision will be whether or not to fish the actual Kenai River. It always offers a strong pull, particularly once there are an appreciable number of sockeye or coho present, as there'll be good-sized rainbows and char following in their wake. If I do choose to fish the Kenai, it will almost always be done in conjunction with a float—either on my large cataraft, or in a smaller fishcat. The Kenai is a big river, and it's not one that allows for wading back-and-forth over long stretches. There are a few sections that I'll hike into and fish when conditions are just right, but I far prefer the flexibility that floating provides.

It's been quite a while since I hiked down into the Kenai canyon; this was a favorite camping destination for my brother and I back in our school days, and one we'd commonly head to whenever we had a break in employment. We'd usually camp on an island in the river, wading across a small side-channel to reach it. I'm can't specifically recall why we'd come to settle on that particular spot, but I'm guessing it may have been in furtherance of a somewhat delusional effort to avoid the copious numbers of brown bears in the area. We'd fish the channels of the main river and had more than a few good conversations around the campfire.

I've always enjoyed getting away from other people, but it turned out we were often not completely alone in this stretch of comparative wilderness. Amidst our earliest explorations of the surrounding area, we ran into a hermit-like, semi-permanent camper who called himself "Forrest," a name uttered with somewhat dubious conviction, and one that I assumed he'd quickly plucked from the air when glancing at the surrounding trees. A self-described pipeliner, he claimed to work the typical four-week-on, two-week-off schedule that's common for North Slope oilfield workers. When it was time for his R&R, Forrest would head for the Kenai, where he seemed to be stashing supplies in various stock-piles across the hillside surrounding his encampment, in preparation for some type of Armageddon that he felt was coming. I'm not sure whatever happened to the guy, which is something one finds themselves saying a lot when talking about the people met upon the fringes of Alaska.

With the majority of my tent camping days behind me, it's far more likely that I'll be gearing up for a float on the river. If that's indeed my plan, the next decision will be to decide which section. While trout can be found throughout the river, the majority of my efforts will take place on its uppermost sections—from the outlet at Kenai lake through the takeout at Jim's Landing, just above the river's entrance to the canyon. There are two nice stretches to float in this upper section, both providing the ideal distance for a half to full-day float, with plenty of time to stop and fish along the way. The midpoint for this upper section is located at the Russian River ferry, providing an ideal spot for put-in or take-out. The number of trout anglers floating these stretches has definitely increased over the past several years, but such a float still provides an experience that'll far exceed anything witnessed at the circus-like mouth of the Russian.

While I'll likely float the Kenai on at least a few occasions over the course of a summer, it's far more likely that I'll be found hiking up a smaller, clear-water tributary in search of the trout and char that invariably shadow the upstream spawners. There are three principal options from which I normally choose when planning for such an excursion; as somewhat of a World War II buff and "Great Escape" fan, I'll stick with the appropriately cryptic labels of Tom, Dick, and Harry.

Tom is a relatively small stream, and—at least for now—doesn't seem to show on too many anglers' radars. I attribute this to the fact that it can be rather difficult to fish at times, running awfully fast during periods of medium to high water. Additionally, large sections of the drainage are extremely tight with surrounding brush, making casting (or even positioning for a proper lie) really tough. It's a fun little creek to explore, though, and it's one of the few that hosts a fairly reliable, residential population of trout even before the salmon arrive. I've done quite well fishing its upper reaches, utilizing a variety of dries and nymphs during the early and mid-seasons. When the sockeye inevitably arrive, the bead fishing can be phenomenal when hit just right, as a good number of seasonal char will move in to join the rainbows as well. On one of my last, late-season sojourns into this particular creek last year, I ran into a fellow fly fisherman emerging from the woods on the trail as I was heading in. I stopped as he drew closer, instantly recognizing the scruffy grin of Wally Adams, whom I'd worked alongside while guiding on the Kulik more than thirty years prior. It was great to catch up, though I was disappointed to learn that he was preparing for an upcoming moving to Texas, of all places, as that scuttled my hopes for any future area exploration with him.

Dick is a slightly larger and significantly slower stream than Tom, moving in a much more meandering manner as it flows towards its outlet. I've been frustrated more than a few times when attempting to prospect this creek during times *other* than the sockeye spawn; the waters are gorgeous, but they often don't seem to be holding any fish. Looking to my past analogous experiences on the waters of Bristol Bay, I'm confident that there *has* to be a period in the spring or early summer when a downward migration of salmon fry should trigger a feeding frenzy close to the creek's mouth, but I have yet to pinpoint it.

It's when the spawning sockeye are finally present, especially through the creek's mid and upper stretches, that this drainage really shines. During a relatively small window in August, a phenomenal number of feisty and determined char will move in to gorge themselves on the eggs of the spawning sockeye, with a lesser number of rainbows always tagging along for good measure. Some of my finest days fishing the Peninsula have been spent on this particular stream, and it's one I always look forward to returning to.

While Tom and Dick are always fun to fish, I tend to hold Harry in particularly high esteem. The largest of these three streams, Harry reminds me a lot of the Brooks River in many of its boulder-filled, tumbling sections, both in size and overall characteristics. While the other two creeks seem to be dominated by dollies during the peak of the sockeye spawn, rainbows reign supreme on the Harry. I've caught some large and powerful fish there—probably the closest I've come to approaching "Katmai conditions" on this side of Cook Inlet. In another similarity to Brooks and its neighboring drainages, I've had to dodge far more brown bears while fishing this particular creek as compared to the other two. In point of fact, I've never even *seen* a brown bear while fishing either Tom or Dick, though I know there are plenty in the area, as evidenced by the copious amount of scat and shredded salmon carcasses that I'm frequently stepping over.

One of the other things that I really enjoy about the Peninsula is the opportunities that it provides for changes in scenery. While the majority of my fishing efforts will center around Cooper Landing and its surrounding drainages, there may be times—particularly as the leaves start assuming their fall colors—when I feel like heading further south. While I don't fish them extensively, the waters of the Ninilchik River, Deep Creek, and the Anchor River offer a good, later-season diversion to fish behind fall, spawning silvers. While there are smaller resident rainbows and transient dollies to be had, it's the presence of larger, ocean-run steelhead that I'll be targeting on these forays. I'll likely not come away with a "high volume" session, but one or two successful hook-ups with these big, powerful fish will qualify the day as an unbridled success.

I haven't even touched on the number of high mountain lakes in the area, most of which boast exceptional populations of arctic grayling. The mountains on the Peninsula are steep, and hikers will often find themselves in for a strenuous jaunt before reaching any sub-alpine benches. I'm primarily a stream guy, but those that are willing to do some hiking in search of a pristine, fish-filled lake will likely find the place all to themselves.

Speaking of solitude, I should probably conclude this regional pro-file by offering one brief disclaimer and cautionary note. For those who wish to travel to the Kenai Peninsula, make sure you do your homework, and that you have realistic expectations regarding the specific locations you've chosen to visit. The waters that I fish are rarely occupied—much less crowded—as I choose to chase trout while the majority of anglers are pursuing bigger (and usually far more plentiful) salmon. This reflects a conscious decision on my part, as—for me—the experience of fishing on a stream entails a hell of a lot more than just catching fish. If you are looking to enjoy a true wilderness experience, and have thus decided to journey to the mouth of the Russian River during the height of the sockeye run, I would respectfully urge you to set this book down for a moment, go to your computer or smartphone, and Google "Kenai combat fishing images." Did you actually do it? If so, excellent. My work here is done. ◉

Chapter Thirteen

MARRIAGE AS A DRY-DROPPER RIG:
Do You Know Which Fly You Are?

My wife Gwen drives a nice little Honda; it's an all-wheel-drive SUV that scoots up and down our hill through the worst of winter conditions, and she knows how to handle it when navigating our road's steep switchbacks. I often find myself riding as her passenger when we head into town on errands, as her rig gets better mileage than my pick-up. I save the truck for when our tasks include hauling water, as there's a large tank strapped into the bed that we use for that particular chore.

Regardless of who's driving, we've developed an instinctive ritual when pulling into the garage at home. Fairbanks is exceedingly dry, especially in the wintertime, with a relative humidity that's comparable with most desert locations (That's why we're far more comfortable in Fairbanks at -30°F than in the coastal town of Anchorage at -10°F, as we laughingly tell our friends to the south: "It's a *dry* cold . . ."). As a result of the excessive dryness, and with conditions commonly exacerbated by the numerous layers of winter clothing that invariably rub together, we've found it necessary to reach over and lightly touch one another with a bare finger, (providing an adequate "ground" for our human circuit) before leaning in for the routinely celebratory, good-to-be-home kiss. Failure to do so inevitably leads to the discharge of a sharp,

static shock across one's lips—contributing to a Pavlovian condition of negative response that I'd rather not reinforce.

When you're together with a person long enough, you eventually figure out what works. I first met Gwen while working as a young police officer in Fairbanks, where she was already serving as an Emergency 911 Dispatcher. For the first three years that I knew her through work, our relationship basically consisted of her telling me where to go, who to see, and what to do. I figured I probably shouldn't mess with the established order of things once we started dating and getting serious. As they say—*If it ain't broke . . .*

I knew that I was defying conventional wisdom in pursuing a romance on the job, though I think it's much more common in emergency services than in many other occupations. When you're working swings or graveyard shifts with midweek days off, it can be hard to find opportunities to socialize with the normal folk. Additionally, the people involved in our line of work are some of the few who realize the true nature (and stressors) of what we see and deal with on a day-in, day-out basis. I know I'm not the first cop to marry a dispatcher, and I likely won't be the last.

We're coming up on our 27th wedding anniversary this summer. I know that probably doesn't qualify as a monumental benchmark for some of the old-timers out there, but I feel like we have a pretty good running start on things. I won't pretend that I have everything solidly figured out at this point, as all the fellow married men out there would surely laugh at such an assertion—and rightly so. I do tend to be somewhat introspective at times, and I've often wondered if I would ever come across some analogy or circumstance that would help me explain to others how I viewed the respective roles in Gwen's and my relationship. It wasn't until a few years ago, while using a guide's services in New Zealand to explore some of their local trout water with a tandem fly setup, that it hit me like a ton of bricks: Our marriage was a classic, dry-dropper arrangement!

Now I'm assuming that many of the people reading this book are flyfishers, and therefore know exactly what a "dry-dropper" refers to. If you haven't fished such a setup, especially at the hands of a guide, then I can only assume you've joined company with the resident caddis larvae and have been living under a rock for the past thirty years. However, I hope you'll indulge me for just a moment as I relate a brief history and evolution of our sport, allowing me to bring the rest of our esteemed readers up to speed.

As most fly fishermen are highly aware, the majority of any trout's diet can be found scurrying about the surface of a stream's bed or drifting amongst its mid-column currents. These food items are generally lumped together and classified as nymphs, to include pupal and larval forms of midges, caddis, stoneflies, and a host of others. Trout tend to hold in water where such items will come floating by or directly to them, allowing them to eat while expending as little energy as possible. Consequently, the savvy nymph fisherman will drift their imitations within close proximity to the lanes of a feeding trout, endeavoring to match the proper depth and drift for each offering. When everything matches up and comes together successfully—bam! Fish on.

There's a minor complication, however. As it turns out, trout and other salmonids can be extraordinarily delicate eaters; a small nymph can be mouthed by the fish, only to be spit back out in such rapid fashion that the angler will have no idea that a take had ever occurred.

Traditional (and recently resurging) "tight-line" nymph fishermen attempt to overcome this problem by keeping as little slack in their lines as possible, attempting to feel every tick and bump of their fly's progress as it bounces along the streambed cobble. The tight-liner will sometimes cheat a bit, using a short, brightly colored length of "sighter material" built into their leader, as that provides a method allowing for the visual recognition of soft takes.

If you have ever fished with an accomplished nymph fisherman, you've likely recognized their superior skillset. Knowledgeable nymph users can almost always out-fish anyone else on a stream, as they're targeting the bulk of their quarry's diet. While it's hard to believe, though, one will often run into individuals on the water that are slightly less than knowledgeable. When a certain, popular fly-fishing movie came out in the early nineties, it was credited with bringing a whole new wave of people to the sport. I suspect that this may indeed be true; what I know for certain is that there suddenly seemed to be a lot more people attempting to fly fish, and many of these folks didn't seem to have the time or patience necessary to learn the intricacies of fishing by feel. Enter the indicator.

The variety of different types of indicators—and their general use—seemed to explode in the 90s. Guides, in particular, likely found that all their newbie clients could be taught to raise their rod tip in a quick hookset much more easily when presented with an easily visible, floatable cue to do so. The use of an indicator became a standard part of the setup for most nymphing rigs; the marginally competent angler could now focus on establishing a proper drift, then simply wait for the telltale twitch of their yarn or Thingamabobber to set the hook.

It's not hard to imagine how the next, inevitable step in the evolutionary process occurred. As guides across the country closely watched while clients drifted indicators in their nymphal pursuits, occasional circumstances would likely arise when a hatch would start to occur, with natural flies being taken on the surface in preference over subsurface offerings. In other cases, a trout may have struck at the angler's indicator, mistaking its silhouette for that of an egg or floating terrestrial. No matter the circumstance, hundreds of guides and experienced anglers across the country likely reached the same, independent conclusion: *"If I'm going to float something on the surface to act as an indicator for my nymph, why not just use a dry fly that might draw its own strikes in the process?"* And . . . hail to the chief . . . the dry-dropper rig rose to quick prominence.

I avoid fishing dry-dropper setups when I can get away with it— usually indicative of those circumstances where a primary food source is so overwhelming (e.g., fish eggs present, a heavy hopper hatch, etc.) that any additional, offered choices are wholly unnecessary. I like to keep track of the minimum number of variables possible, and I *hate* undoing tangles . . . particularly if a split-shot is involved. However, when one needs to cover a lot of water, and *especially* when one's trying to figure out what's being eaten, prospecting with a dry-dropper rig is hard to beat. It simply allows one to cover more bases, often significantly accelerating the determination as to what the day's favorite fly is going to be, allowing for the secondary offering to then be ditched if desired.

So . . . we should now all be on the same page when it comes to dry-droppers; but how could that possibly pertain to marriage? Well, if you've ever fished such a setup—and paid any attention to what was being accomplished in the process—then you might already start to catch some of my drift. (Sorry; I promised my wife that I'd scale-back on my fish puns, once I'd left school. . . .)

When fishing a dry-dropper rig, one no longer relies upon a single fly drifting along amongst the currents, venturing forth in solitary pursuit of its life's intended mission. Rather, there are now two flies being fished—working together in a closely coordinated fashion—in an effort to achieve success and the happiness that results. The flies are commonly quite different from one another in many respects, and it's often the result of this purposefully paired dissimilarity that contributes to the overall setup's success. The relationship can sometimes get a bit messy, as keeping things flowing smoothly with a minimum of tangles is inherently more difficult when fishing two flies as opposed to one. However, when done correctly and pursued with continuous good faith, the results will likely far eclipse that of the single fly's solitary journey.

The two flies comprising a dry-dropper setup have obviously different roles. The dry fly that floats along the surface often provides an overall sense of visible direction, and its presence will invariably draw additional opportunities to the relationship—sometimes resulting in the most prized catch of the day. Often unseen as it toils beneath the surface, the dropper may frequently be doing the lion's share of the work; it sometimes doesn't seem to be as highly recognized or appreciated in its underwater role, until such time that it hooks a fine fish for retrieval. Both flies are critical to the pair's overall success, and neither should assume an attitude of prominence or superiority.

When one accepts my offered premise, the next question from married folks logically follows: *"O.K., if my relationship is that of a dry-dropper, which one am I?"* This seemingly innocuous inquiry quickly cuts to the heart of the matter, as the dynamics between two flies fished in coordinated fashion can alter considerably over the course of a single drift, much less throughout an entire day's angling efforts. The easiest way to illustrate the common characteristics—and potential pitfalls— of each fly's performance will lie in an examination of specific potential circumstances, which I'll enumerate shortly. However, before proceeding, please allow me to declare this one, important caveat: When I speak of a failing on the part of either fly (or use the word "spouse" in any accompanying analogy) this should be strictly interpreted to mean "Daniel Hoffman, the clueless husband" when viewed within the context of my own relationship. I'm assuming that Gwen may read this book at some point in the future, so I just wanted to make sure and throw that out there. . . .

PROBLEM AREA #1:
USING A DRY FLY OF INSUFFICIENT BUOYANCY.

The dry fly used in a tandem setup will normally catch fewer fish than its subsurface partner, and that's often by design. The fact that the dry isn't the primary "fish-catcher" should in no way diminish the importance of its overall role. By floating on the surface, and in maintaining the direct connection to its partner underneath, the dry fly will provide the subtle cues necessary for the nymph to achieve success. A small midge pattern fished through the currents can be inhaled and spit out dozens of times over the course of a day; if the dry doesn't do its job and provide an indication for the subsurface takes, then their partner is likely working for naught.

In consideration for this role, the dry fly that's chosen to serve as an indicator *must* be up to the task, possessing the character and qualities necessary to maintain its sense of floatation and purpose—even through choppy waters. Prospective nymphal spouses would do well to choose their dry partners carefully; the daintiest of floating patterns may look quite flashy in the fly shop's display case, but will likely succumb to submersion when faced with the currents of real life. The true "indicator-dry" will remain steadfast and buoyant through the roughest of conditions, contributing to the partnership's ongoing success.

PROBLEM #2:
USING A DROPPER THAT'S
TOO MUCH OF A LIGHTWEIGHT.

As reflected above, the largely unseen role of the dropper is no less important. The dropper will normally assume the task of catching the most fish, or, at the very least, provide the necessary prospecting and exploration necessary to chart the pair's continued course through the stream. There's a reason that the dropper rides below the surface—that's where the fish are.

However, in order to be a truly effective partner, the dropper cannot simply posture at success by merely slipping below the surface. The dropper needs to work at the correct depth, as the dry deserves far more in a partner than the feigned efforts of a mere poser.

While many natural nymphs can be found at varying depths throughout the water column, particularly when dealing with emergent phases, many are commonly found near the bottom where they live and become frequently detached. One can fish the finest nymph reproductions out there, but if those offerings are sailing high over the heads of the trout that are feeding at depth, then the dropper's efforts are futile at best—and, at their worst, may actually represent a purposeful display of disingenuous sincerity. It's the job of the nymph to get down and do the hard work, wherever it's necessary. If unwilling or unable to do so, then a different partner should've perhaps been chosen.

PROBLEM AREA #3:
USING A DROPPER THAT'S TOO HEAVY.

Just as using a dropper that's too light will lead to a highly diminished chance for success, so too shall that of a nymph that's too heavily weighted for prevailing conditions. As referenced previously, many natural nymphs and emergers will commonly ride the mid-depth currents, often rising to even higher levels as they prepare to breach the film. If one attempts to throw a heavily weighted offering amid such conditions, it's likely that the prospective meal will drift well below any feeding trout, failing to draw any strikes in the process. Worse yet, the overweight nymph will likely get hung up on the stream's bottom with frustrating regularity, further complicating what should otherwise be a happy relationship between the two tandem flies.

Within the context of the marital analogy, however, the most serious consequence manifesting from such a condition can result when the dry is unintentionally drug beneath the surface by its overweight and singularly focused dropper. It's the job of the nymph to work *with* its partner, not to drown it. For those circumstances when it's necessary for the dropper to seek or maintain greater depth, then it's incumbent upon the angler to make an honest adjustment with the dry, ensuring the health and survivability of both partners.

PROBLEM #4:
COMPLICATING THE RIG
WITH UNNECESSARY WEIGHT.

It has often been said that the difference between a good fisherman and a great one is a single split-shot, and for good reason. When considering how to fish one's dropper in a tandem rig, it's critical to get the nymph down to the proper level in the water column, which can often mean the addition or subtraction of shot as necessary. However, despite its benefits, the inevitable motion of a shot freely swinging on one's leader when airborne produces its share of complications.

As I've alluded to before, I hate tangles. I don't curse often—but when faced with the pendulum-swinging, in-your-face movement of a gyrating split-shot while I attempt to resolve what had started out as a simple tangle—well, it's at that point that I sometimes find myself stretching the limits of my vocabulary. Fishing two flies is complicated enough for me, and I'll avoid adding extra, mid-tippet weight whenever possible. If I do need to add a shot, I'll use the minimum amount necessary to achieve results, or consider switching to a dropper with a more properly weighted body. One should avoid adding additional complications to the relationship between two tandem flies whenever possible.

PROBLEM AREA #5:
INTRODUCING A THIRD FLY INTO THE MIX.

Sorry, but you're going to have to head to a different type of bookstore if you're looking for a story extolling the benefits of three-fly setups. The standard dry-dropper rig works quite well, as it allows the angler to manage two committed partners in tandem, keeping any extraneous elements to an absolute minimum. For anyone who has already subscribed to the applicability of this overall analogy, I doubt that anything further need be said.

Speaking of wrapping things up, it's probably time for me to do the same. I should likely ask Gwen if we need to jump in the car and head down the hill, as we're getting short on a few grocery items in our pantry. It shouldn't take long, but we'll need to grab our heavy jackets, as it's looking fairly chilly outside. I'm not sure yet, but when we get home and pull into the garage, I may just decide to roll the dice and forgo the standard "grounding touch" before leaning over to give her a quick smooch. I don't ever want to become *too* predictable, after all, and I'm always looking for ways to maintain the spark in our relationship. ◉

Chapter Fourteen

SPECIAL PLACES #3:
Katmai

While Colorado will always hold a special place in my heart, I'll forever be grateful to my father for having had the courage to pack up our family and move us to Alaska when I was still quite young. This state has provided me with an untold wealth of opportunities, both fishing and otherwise, most of which I would've surely missed out on if we'd stayed in the Lower 48.

And while there are myriad, wondrous locations to see and experience here—each perhaps deserving of their own chapter or book—none is more deserving of my own "special places" designation than Katmai.

Sandwiched between the waters of Lake Iliamna to the north and Becharof to the south, the boundaries of Katmai National Park and Preserve encompass an area exceeding 6,300 square miles, larger in size than the entire State of Connecticut. Anchoring the base of the Alaska Peninsula, the waters of Katmai flow both eastward to the waters of Shelikof Strait and Cook Inlet in the Pacific, as well as westward to the tidal expanses of Bristol Bay in the Bering Sea.

Lying within a circum-Pacific zone of notable seismic activity, the landscape is one truly born of fire and ice. The steam escaping from active volcanoes rises harmlessly, quickly evaporating over their

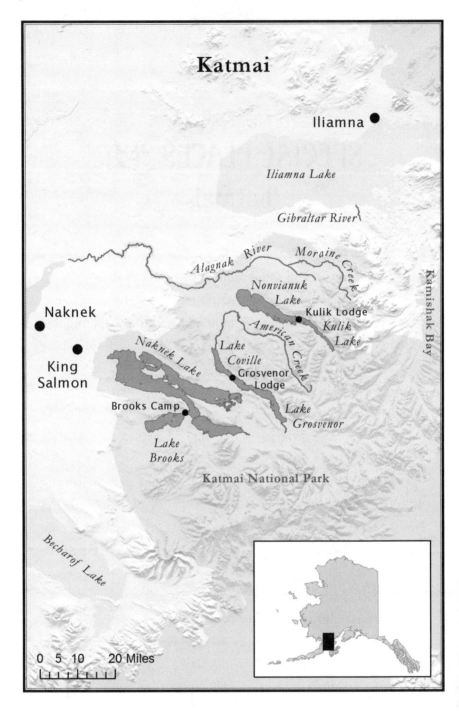

Katmai

Iliamna

Iliamna Lake

Gibraltar River

Alagnak River

Moraine Creek

Kamishak Bay

Nonvianuk Lake

Naknek

Kulik Lodge

Kulik Lake

American Creek

Naknek Lake

Lake Coville

Grosvenor Lodge

King Salmon

Brooks Camp

Lake Grosvenor

Lake Brooks

Katmai National Park

Becharof Lake

0 5 10   20 Miles

glacially-capped peaks, yet provides an ever-present reminder of the geologic turmoil residing just beneath the surface.

The threat evidenced by the region's sulfur-laden fumaroles is not idle—nor should it be taken lightly. The most cataclysmic volcanic eruption of the twentieth century was recorded in Katmai in June of 1912, estimated to be ten times as powerful as that of the 1980 Mt. Saint Helens event. The multiday eruption sent an unfathomable amount of ash into the air, paralyzing the community of Kodiak some 100 miles to the east. The island's residents struggled for days in complete, choking darkness, with some of their rooftops collapsing under the weight of accumulating ashfall. The amount of volcanic material displaced through the Novarupta volcano was so great, its reservoir of magma (drawn from underneath nearby Mt. Katmai) caused the latter to collapse in on itself. Heavy flows of pyroclastic material cascaded downward, filling the Knife Creek and Ukak River drainages with molten rock and ash hundreds of feet deep, creating what's now known as the Valley of 10,000 smokes.

When one visits the Valley today, it still presents itself as a rather surreal and otherworldly moonscape. One can watch the roaring waters of the Ukak as it continues to carve its path through buttresses of solidified ash and rock, with the faintest fringes of bordering vegetation just now beginning to slowly creep back onto the edges of the valley floor. Many of the fishermen visiting the region will likely never travel to the Valley, though there are plenty of other reminders to invoke the fiery recollections of Katmai's past.

As one flies over the outstretched fingers of Naknek Lake, the difference in clarity between its Iliuk arm and the remainder of the body is notable. While drainages such as the Brooks, Idavain, and Margot Creek add their clear waters to the mix, the Savanoski and Ukak Rivers continue to deposit the bulk of volcanic sediments found within the basin. Landing on Naknek's shore at Brooks Camp, one immediately notes the presence of floating pumice rock, newly deposited upon the beach with every easterly wind.

(Helpful Katmai hint #1: If you ever find yourself on the beach at Brooks, and you're in close proximity to an amphibious plane getting ready to turn lakeward, make sure to stay well away from its blowback zone. Pumice rock is extraordinarily light and acts as an excellent sand-blasting agent.)

In stark contrast to the area's volcanically affected zones, the richness and abundance of life evidenced throughout the remainder of the region is staggering. Rivers and lakefronts abound with shorebirds and water-fowl, all of whom migrate to the area to take advantage of its summer riches. Wolves and moose can be found throughout the region, though it's sometimes hard to believe that any calves from the latter can survive to maturity, given the number of intently focused predators that hunt the area.

(Helpful Katmai hint #2: If you ever find yourself around Brooks in early June and happen to have a cow moose with a newborn calf come running past, get the hell out of the way. It's virtually guaranteed that a brown bear is fast on their heels, and they will be huffing along any second. . . .)

And yes, there are the bears. Perhaps the definitive characteristic of Katmai's waterways, the bears seem to be everywhere. Not so much so in the early spring, as they tend to scatter through the higher country once emerging from their dens in the spring. But—once the sockeye start to push their way forth into the various drainages—one may as well chime a cruise ship's dinner bell, announcing that the evening buffet has been spread. The bears start coming . . . and they keep coming. Congregating in unbelievable numbers along fish-choked streams and majestic falls, these normally solitary bruins tolerate one another in close proximity for a relatively short time each season, as the caloric incentive for them to do so far outweighs their normally territorial instincts. I've never seen a black bear in Katmai, and I doubt one would survive for long. The brown bear is the king of the country, and everyone knows it.

Throughout the course of the sockeye spawn, the brown bears will congregate at well-known chokepoints, to include such famous locations as the McNeil River and Brooks River Falls. Away from the throngs of photographers and tourists, there are many other, not-so-famous locations that'll draw bears in equally high numbers. I can vividly remember the very last time I flew into the upper reaches of Gibraltar Creek, guiding a group of Kulik clients for the late season rainbow fishery. As our pilot performed a slow, circular reconnoiter, allowing us to scan the roughly half-mile interval that we planned to fish after hiking from a nearby landing site, I counted twenty-eight brown bears plying that particular salmon-filled stretch. Deciding that discretion indeed constitutes the better part of valor, we decided to hit-up the neighboring drainage instead.

(Helpful Katmai hint #3: When fishing streams of extremely high bear density, the only way to do so is to exit the water whenever a bear comes along, giving them as wide a berth as possible while they focus on finding their next fish. I've found the uppermost acceptable limit for such concentrations to be around twenty bears per mile; any more than that, and you'll spend your entire day simply dodging bears while getting very little fishing done.)

As the season progresses, the bears get fatter and fatter, amassing weight of unbelievable proportion as they prepare for their next winter's sleep. People have often asked me if it's unduly concerning—or down-right scary—to fish amongst such high concentrations of bears; truth be told, it really isn't. While one always needs to maintain a high degree of awareness, maintaining a healthy level of respect and taking all sensible precautions, the bottom line is that the bears really couldn't give a rat's ass about the puny humans who occasionally stumble along the waters. Just as trout get highly attuned to a specific emerger or color of egg, so too have the bears become completely hyper-focused on the presence of spawning salmon. If one allows them free and unfettered access to their food source, staying well away from any mother's cubs, there's very little to worry about.

(Helpful Katmai hint #4: The bears around Brooks get so fat in the fall, they'll dig a depression into the softness of Naknek's lakeshore before laying down, providing a pressure-free recess for their excessive bellies to settle into. With legs often splayed front and rearward, these bears blend quite well into their pumice-filled, sandy surroundings. If you should ever find yourself working the early morning coffee duty at the lodge and decide to take a shortcut by shuffling down the beach on a gray, drizzly morning before fully waking up, nearly stepping upon the head of a slumbering brown bear is a surefire way to achieve instant daytime clarity . . . a fact to which I can personally attest.)

If I seem to be leaving something out, don't worry; I've obviously saved the best for last.

Yes, this is a book about fly fishing, and the opportunities offered throughout Katmai are truly among the best—if not the *very* best—to be found in the entire world. If you're interested in casting for salmon of every Pacific species, options abound. If you've always wanted to catch an arctic grayling or northern pike, the region has got you covered. Arctic char and lake trout? Prepare for a trip that you'll never forget. However, while I may tend toward exclusivity in some of my personal orientations, it's hard for me to wrap my head around the fact that anyone could ever come out to Katmai without having rainbows as their primary focus.

The rainbows of Katmai are . . . well . . . they're just *different*. I've never spoken with a fisheries biologist to see if genetic studies have been done specific to the region, but I suspect that the rainbows in many of the drainages bear far more similarities to true, ocean-swimming steelhead than those of lifetime, river residents. I make this assumption based upon my own observations of the streams that I've fished, many of which exhibit a highly pronounced degree of seasonality.

Some of the largest and most powerful trout that I've managed to hook have been found in the uppermost reaches of Katmai's interior drainages, in creeks like the Moraine, Gibraltar, and Funnel.

*(Helpful Katmai tip #5: If you ever have an opportunity to fish the above drainages, make **absolutely sure** that you have a sufficient amount of high-quality, braided Dacron backing beneath your fly line. The biggest 'bows of these drainages can literally smoke your reel's gears in mere milliseconds, taking you far into that thinnest of lifelines.)*

The crystalline waters of these streams come alive for the most intense (but all too brief) window in late summer and early fall, when the spawning sockeye finally manage to navigate their way to the creek's headwaters. The streams are all but barren for the remainder of the year, as the big rainbows back their way down into the sheltering waters of lakes like the Battle, Kukaklek, Nonvianuk, and Coville. The rich depths of these intermediate reservoirs likely provide a dietary environment similar to that of a true ocean, allowing the rainbows to achieve a size comparable to that of their steely cousins.

As to the rainbow's . . . um . . . attitude? Well, you've got me there. It's hard to describe or fully articulate, but there's just *something* notably different in the degree of contempt evidenced and the total, incredulous indignation that a Katmai rainbow displays upon feeling the first sting of betrayal when mouthing an egg-bead. Immediately ripping off line in a frenzy of unbridled explosiveness, nearly every angler who's ever fished there has—at least once—experienced the initial panic immediately following a hook-set, thinking *"My God! What fresh hell have I unleashed?!!"*

Luckily, one needn't restrict their pursuit of 'bows to the late season, egg-pattern fisheries. Early and mid-season streamer fishing in the Brooks, Kulik, Alagnak, and other rivers of the region will provide more than enough excitement, where a sculpin or leech stripped across the bottom will inevitably produce a strike of bone-jarring proportion. During the mid-weeks of June, swarms of sockeye smolt descending down into the lakes from upper drainages will cause a frenzy of feeding activity amongst the local trout populations. Fishing sparsely tied, Thunder Creek–type patterns in the surface film will produce nonstop action, particularly when fishing the lower portions of the rivers near their lakefront mouths.

The areas at the river mouths can also be surprisingly productive for large lake trout as well, who (unlike most of their deep-water compatriots elsewhere) commonly stage in shallower water to feed from the river's outflowing bounty throughout the course of the summer. One can wade out to fish the outgoing current of the Kulik into the maw of the Nonvianuk, allowing a light-colored bunny leech (fished on a sink-tip line) time to reach depth at the end of its swing. Stripping the leech jerkily inward results in an almost guaranteed strike, with leviathans of substantial proportion often being brought to the net.

(Helpful Katmai tip #6: While always a tempting solo activity to pursue in the evenings, this wading option should likely be abandoned in the latter part of the season. The small islands and paths at the mouth of the Kulik become a favorite location for the local fishing bears, and one could find themselves stuck out in the lake for quite some time.)

As noted previously, rainbows aren't the only game in town, and I suppose I shouldn't let my own preferential orientations overshadow the other opportunities found in and around Katmai—particularly when it comes to salmon. Flowing westward out of the park toward its confluence with the Kvichak, the Alagnak River represents one of the largest "salmon factories" in the region, allowing one to fish for any Pacific species desired. Fishing the Kvichak itself, where one could travel upstream all the way to its source at Lake Illiamna if desired, one can find silver salmon in a quantity and energy that'll result in complete exhaustion. Head yet a bit further west, and you'll find yourself in the prime of king country, where massive chinooks can be had in the waters of the Nushagak.

One thing that I always enjoyed about fishing and guiding out of Katmai was the flexibility that the location provided with respect to weather. Given its central location at the base of the Peninsula, one could always head to the opposite coast if foul weather was forecast. When the Bristol Bay drainages mentioned above were due to be socked-in from Bering Sea storm systems, heading east to the drainages of Kamishak Bay on the Pacific side of the Peninsula often offered a sunny alternative.

The Kamishak River provides excellent flyfishing for ocean-fresh silver and chum salmon, with smaller drainages in the vicinity providing for excellent hike-in, sight-fishing opportunities on smaller waters.

*(Helpful Katmai hint #7: The coastal brown bears that prowl many of the smaller creeks of Western Cook Inlet are not as habituated to the presence of humans than those of more frequently-visited locations. If you're going to spend the day fishing silvers and are looking to take a few back with you, restrict any takes 'til your last thirty minutes of fishing. These are **not** streams where you want to be dragging a dead salmon around with you all day long. . . .)*

I didn't make it over to the Pacific side as often as I would've liked to, but it seemed that every time I did, something special would occur. On one of my last coho trips of the season, I was hiking back out to the beach with my clients when we heard a bit of a ruckus toward the river's mouth. Emerging from the brush, we watched a brown bear chase a full-grown, bull caribou out into the ocean surf of Cook Inlet. I'd rarely seen a caribou kicking around this portion of the low country, as most would commonly be seen as we flew over the upper benches—clustered atop the remaining patches of snow as they sought refuges against the hordes of ever-present mosquitos. The bull, still in full velvet during the late summer month, easily swam away from the bear's reach once in deeper water. I had never carried any kind of video camera when guiding, and this was long before the days of smartphones. I doubt that any film clip could recapture the clarity of the moment that remains within my mind, though, and I suppose that's the best place for it.

If there's one other, non-fishing memory that'll always remain from my guiding days out at Kulik, it'd be learning to water ski on the frigid waters of Nonvianuk Lake. Longtime Maintenance Manager Harry Wehrman always kept a few skis stashed away in the recesses of his shop, and on the hottest evenings of summer he'd break them out for the lodge staff to try behind the largest of his inboard jets—the boat we lovingly referred to as "the Camaro." I'd never water skied before, but as a lifelong downhill skier I was able to get up quickly on my first attempt, strongly encouraged to do so by the 40-degree water. I can't speak to the normalcy of the "standard waterskiing experience," but skimming over the outlet of the Kulik River in the late evening sun—with tens of thousands of staging sockeye streaking outward in every direction as I passed overhead—well, that's a mental image that'll always stay with me.

I had said before that I was concerned I may have been "spoiled for life" by extensively fishing Katmai in my earlier years, and in some ways I certainly have been. I'll gladly take that burden, however, as the angling memories that've already been deposited into my lifetime account constitute a gift that *far* outweighs any frustrations or comparative disappointments that I might experience at other locations in the future. I've fished both sides of its coast, and I have flown into its most remote, interior drainages. The waters of Katmai have been indelibly imprinted upon my consciousness, and my life remains far richer for it.

While I haven't been able to make it back out there very often, Gwen and I were able to bring my folks out to celebrate their 50th wedding anniversary in 2011, taking them to see the bears of Brooks Falls and the Valley of 10,000 Smokes, as well as fishing the waters of the Kulik and American in celebration. I was able to bring my father back out a few years later for his last Alaskan fishing trip, spending a few very special days with the staff at Kulik—and with Ray Irvine over at Grosvenor—as Dad was now doing a bit more lake fishing than he would've done in the past.

Just this past fall, my best friend Glen and I were able to take advantage of a late-season special that Kulik Lodge offered for Alaska residents, given the number of travel cancellations incurred as a result of the COVID pandemic. The autumn egg-drop was in full swing, and the rainbow fishing we experienced on the Kulik and American was better than anything I'd experienced thirty years prior. The trip really filled me with hope and optimism for Katmai's continued health, as it was clearly apparent that decades of responsible, catch-and-release management is clearly fulfilling its role.

If one is a true theater buff, then I suppose a pilgrimage to Broadway is inevitable. As a longtime Denver Broncos fan, I was lucky enough to attend Elway's final Superbowl, and found the entire experience to be highly worthwhile. Within that same vein, but at a measurement of infinitely greater magnitude, I would urge *anyone* who has pursued a life of flyfishing to GET THEE OUT TO KATMAI, especially while you're still young enough to fully enjoy it. There are no guarantees that the landscape will last forever, and I'm a strong proponent of the notion that we're only granted a single lifetime to experience the wonders of this earth. If you need to work on squirreling away some extra savings in order to make the trip, get started now.

Whatever the inevitable costs, you'll find it to be well worth it. ⊙

PART FOUR

In Comfortable Waders

Chapter Fifteen

SEEKING A LIFE OF DRAG-FREE DRIFT
Mending When Necessary to Keep it All Together

I t's sometimes easy for me to forget that everyone isn't living their lives in the same manner that I do, framing the parameters of existence through their own evolving journey as fly fishermen. Well, I suppose that's not entirely accurate . . . it's often pretty easy to remember, once people open their mouths and start talking. Oh well, I suppose everyone carries their own perspectives in life, coming to their own conclusions as to how best manage the baffling array of situations and decisions that spring forth on a daily basis.

While it's sometimes tempting for me to hop on my soapbox and advocate for the superiority of the angler's approach, I hesitate to do so. Spending time at Sylvan Lake with my grandfather taught me the folly of judging lake fishermen, and I suppose I should carry that spirit somewhat further forward. I do recognize that there are meaningful avocations in life other than fly fishing, and that individuals may develop their own equally profound, existential frameworks through their pursuit of varying alternatives.

It's hard, though. When I see advertisements for all the "reality" TV shows out there, (Many of which, coincidentally, attempt to portray life here in Alaska—with laughably poor results . . .) it makes me wonder why on earth people wouldn't want to just go outside and *live* for themselves, rather than watching others experience the joys of experiential life on television. It's the same with virtual reality; companies like *Oculus* will spend billions of dollars over the coming years developing and marketing computerized headsets, allowing people to spend their free time and energies completely immersing themselves in simulated worlds and situations, where the sum total of life's success can be measured by the point-score at the end of the game.

Yes, everyone has their perspectives—though some carry more weight with me than others. As I prepared to write this book, I was discussing its proposed theme with my hunting buddy Randy. As soon as I mentioned the phrase "drag-free drift," he immediately asserted that he knew exactly where I was going with the analogy, then proceeded to recount his vivid recollections from a float-hunt we had done together several years ago on Alaska's Sheenjek River.

There had been precious little rain that summer, and the water that flowed through the stream's multiple, braided channels was at its lowest level in years. Dirk Nickisch with *Coyote Air* out of Coldfoot had flown us into the far upper reaches of the drainage, and—after assembling the frame, inflating the pontoons, and packing our gear into my 16-foot cataraft—we had our work cut out for us as we spent the next nine days picking and choosing amongst the numerous, shallow forks encountered as we headed downstream. Many stretches required us to jump out and half-carry, half-pull the raft over lengthy expanses of exposed gravel, trying to minimize the wear and tear on the pontoon's lower surfaces. It wasn't until the fifth day of the trip that we finally found ourselves in consistent, floatable water.

It's funny; the thought of the comparable rafting analogy had never even occurred to me prior to that conversation, but it was obvious that—while struggling through those first, challenging days on the upper Sheenjek—finding a drag-free drift (for our boat) had indeed become our primary focus. My oversight of the obvious comparison was perhaps even more noteworthy due to the other similarities involved. Both the drifting fly and bobbing raft are looking to forge their own paths down a river. Moreover, success will largely be determined by the degree of anticipation displayed by the person in control. When looking far ahead to an upcoming fork, the oarsmen need make but a small, mid-channel adjustment to send the craft down the right path. Conversely, even a small period of inattention can often lead to a flurry of exhaustive, last-minute efforts, struggling to overcome prevailing currents in an attempt to gain the proper channel. (Or, worse yet, realizing an error too late . . . and finding oneself headed down the wrong fork.)

While the rafting analogy is indeed comparable in many respects, I'll continue to embrace that of the fly, thoughtfully cast upon a stream's flowing waters. As referenced previously, not all flies are necessarily intended to follow a free-flowing path. However, most of the ones I commonly fish seem destined to do so. Whether fishing an egg-pattern or bead along the bottom, drifting a small nymph through the mid-column currents, or visually tracking the dance of a dry as it navigates the surface, my offerings are intended to blend seamlessly with the natural world that flows along with them.

The fisherman is faced with several choices before the fly is even sent forward, much less those presented during its subsequent drift. It's through the evaluation of all factors involved, and—perhaps most importantly—*in anticipation of likely consequences*—that the angler makes initial and continuous adjustments throughout the course of his fly's journey. It is only through this process of careful consideration and deliberative adjustment that the fly fisherman can truly hope to achieve a drag-free drift.

PRE-CAST CONSIDERATIONS AND ADJUSTMENTS

Before an angler even makes their first cast, there are several crucial factors to be examined in hopes of achieving a proper drift. So too, in life, can one pause in deliberation before making decisions that result in travel down a particular path. At this early point in my writing process, I don't know whether this book will be published in hardback or soft-cover. I'm truly hoping for the former, though, as I anticipate a time in the near future when a prospective reader will say "Yeah, I can see it! It's all about going with the flow . . ." at which point I'll desperately want the option of smacking them upside their head with the more substantial, hardbound version.

Please allow me to be perfectly clear on this point: Achievement of a drag-free drift in life does *NOT* result from one's ability to "go with the flow." In fact, it's quite the opposite. One only need to spend a few minutes walking streamside to see the amount of hopelessly stranded flotsam swirling about in the eddies, or that of other stream-born debris hung up along the banks, to see where such a philosophy can lead. Many of these castaways happily went with the flow, confident that they were doing OK as long as they were headed downstream in some fashion. Others may have been swept into unwanted currents, despite their best efforts. For the purposely cast fly, however, neither circumstance should ever manifest itself if the angler is paying attention.

Before the first cast is made, one should determine whether they're even in the proper water. As I'd mentioned before, my home river presents some wonderful options to catch some magnificent grayling. However, I'd face inevitable disappointment if I expended a day's effort on that stream in hopes of catching a rainbow. If one wants to be in a position to achieve success, they had better know what it looks like in the first place.

Assuming that the angler has targeted the correct species, there are numerous additional considerations that'll require deliberation before the first fly is cast. Has the fisherman put in the time and study necessary to make good, informed decisions regarding his/her proposed methods? It'll be difficult to achieve a drag-free drift with a dry if one only brought their streamer box and sink-tip line. Similarly, one's nymphing efforts may be doomed if a small vial of split-shot was inadvertently left at home. Just as a fisherman should be fully (and correctly) equipped before wading into the waters, so too should anyone be prepared with the requisite set of tools and knowledge before embarking upon any effort of significance.

When the knowledgeable and properly equipped angler sets foot in the stream, all the perfect casts in the world may still be for naught if the right holding water hasn't been targeted. It's sometimes all too easy to confuse any type of spurious motion or activity with that of actual, meaningful work. Most of us have limited budgets of time, attention, and energy, none of which should be expended in wasted effort. Again, one needs to know what truly constitutes success before it can be effectively pursued in a targeted manner. Figure out where your prey actually lies, then you can work on fishing directly towards that water.

There is one last major, pre-cast consideration that the angler should address: If I hook a fish, am I in position to successfully handle it? As the saying goes, be careful what you wish for- as you may end up getting it. It's often quite surprising to see how many people are shocked—and sadly unprepared—when encountering that first moment of realization that their intended efforts have met with success, only to find out that the outcome wasn't as desirable as they'd hoped for. This goes to the heart of a major component of my "drag-free drift" philosophy: The importance of *knowing oneself* and *anticipating* how a future event will ultimately be received.

147

As he frequently does, (while often having no idea he's doing so . . .) my dad provides a great example. Most of our family, to include all my siblings and their spouses and kids, are on social media to at least some degree. It's an easy way to stay connected across states and continents, sharing photos and updates as we endeavor to maintain our close connections with each other. Not Dad. It used to irk me to some degree, as—after putting together a nice post with photographs to share across family groups—I'd have to copy those same photos and paste the text into a separate email, all so that I could share the same information with him. I tried numerous times over the course of several visits to offer some "helpful tutorials" and get him set up on a proper platform, but he simply wouldn't have any of it.

It wasn't until we had a deeper discussion on the matter that I came to realize the source of his resistance. As Dad explained, (and as I really should've already known . . .) he doesn't handle stress very well, and there are a lot of "little things" that can easily send him into a state of anxiety or mild depression. And—regardless of how well one attempts to set up boundaries and permissions on social media groups—there exists the probable opportunities for political commentary and other troublesome issues to occasionally interject themselves into such online exchanges.

Well, as it turns out, Dad's smart enough to truly *know himself,* and he could *anticipate* the problems that would likely arise from attempting to participate in such forums. As such, he made the conscious decision to seek a drag-free drift for that part of his life, rather than allowing his dry-fly to be pulled hurriedly downstream by an uncontrolled belly of line. All of us kids still talk with him just as freely on the phone and through email, and I no longer mind creating the occasional, duplicate communication. I figure it's a rather small price to pay in exchange for his overall peace and happiness. If I had to conclude this section by offering a singular piece of distilled advice, it would be this: Determine those conditions that lead to unwelcome "drama" in your life and figure out how to ditch them.

POST-CAST ADJUSTMENTS

While the mechanics of actual mending can seem a bit more complicated, taking care of the pre-cast adjustments will have already laid most of the groundwork towards one's success. Once again, *anticipation* is key—and one's initial mending efforts may often be worked right into the cast itself. It can be somewhat foolish to let a length of line land upon the water, if one knows ahead of time that an immediate adjustment will then need to be made. Similarly, when pursuing a goal in life, an adjustment to one's approach should be made at the *first instant* that a need for change is recognized. Otherwise, one is simply destined to waste energy on follow-up, corrective measures that shouldn't have been needed in the first place.

When fishing dry flies upstream to feeding trout, one could potentially cast directly over the top of the fish, allowing the fly to then drift back downstream to them. When the line first lands upon the water, a mend to the left or right will keep its bulk from passing over the fish's heads, presumably presenting a less disruptive and threatening profile. However, in allowing the line to hit the surface and then making the highly visible mend, it's far more likely that you've already spooked your quarry. Those that anticipate such circumstances will be much better served by simply taking a few steps to one side or the other, changing the angle of their presentation to avoid any cast-over of line. Similarly, the more adept angler could simply perform a "reach cast," delivering a sideways mend in midair, thus allowing the line to fall undetected outside of the fish's feeding lane.

The next type of adjustment that's most commonly addressed in these types of corrective discussions involves the necessity to mend the midportion of one's line back upstream, as faster, mid-stream currents often cause a U-shaped "belly" to form, inevitably drawing the fly downstream at a rate faster than the prevailing current. Thankfully, the use of a floating line and/or use of an indicator provides an easily recognizable, visible cue that such a circumstance is occurring. The angler who's focused on his line and paying attention can easily spot the situation at its earliest stages of development, making the necessary mend to allow for the fly's continued, drag-free drift. For the most competent of fly fishermen, the development will be *anticipated*, with the corrective mend occurring a few seconds before it's actually needed.

So too, in life, are we normally presented with clear, recognizable cues that we're being drawn away from a drag-free drift. If one is truly paying attention, corrective action can be taken to keep one's efforts on a proper path, often initiated at a point that will preclude any undesirable effects. It's unreasonable to always try and assume a state of hypervigilance, though, and it's likely that there will be times when one looks up to see that a pronounced belly of line has already formed, pulling the hapless fly downstream. It's at this point that one's experience, judgement, and overall character comes into play. If the path of the drift is both promising and salvageable, then an immediate, corrective mend should be made. The angler will have likely lost a small window of opportunity during the midpart of the drift, but there are still fish that can likely be caught through its lower portions.

Conversely, if one judges that they've completely blown the drift, the wisest course of action may be to draw the entire line quickly off the water, before the rapidly sweeping fly can streak downstream and potentially spook the tail-end feeders. No one likes to give up after an initial expenditure of effort, but one should always try and keep the big-picture perspective in view. While it's not necessary (or helpful) to beat oneself up over making an initial mistake, the error should not be compound by failing to take decisive, corrective action when warranted.

The final mend that's worth discussing deals with upstream drag, most often encountered towards the end of a drift as one's line begins to straighten. The angler who's paying attention will often discern that a highly desirable portion of water may still be in reach, provided that his fly continues to drift on its current path. A strong downstream mend can deliver an extra portion of line—and accompanying slack—at this point, allowing the fly to continue its natural, drag-free drift for several more feet. It's uncanny how many times this will result in a strike; I surmise this is likely the result of fish who've tracked the fly from further upstream, finally making the decision to go for the take in those last, critical feet.

The benefits and analogy of the downstream mend will hopefully be recognized by the students of this discussion. While one may have already established what appears to be a solid, drag-free drift in life, continued success shouldn't be taken for granted. It's often when things are already going well that a small portion of additional, applied effort can result in truly extraordinary gains. If one is on solid footing—and has the available line in-hand to do so—go ahead and throw an additional coil downstream. The further extension provided to your drift may just result in your best catch of the day.

ADDRESSING SNAGS AND TANGLES

I keep asking you folks to pay attention. Well, if you've done so through the course of this book, you should feel quite comfortable in the knowledge that this author doesn't have everything neatly figured out. I continue to deal with my fair share of snags, tangles, and other midstream mishaps, but I suppose that's what constitutes real life. Fishing in the absence of such hazards would cause this sport to quickly devolve into one of inferiority for me, as I feel it's the anticipation of (and approach to) such hazards that has factored so prominently in the development of my own "angler's perspective" and approach to life's unique challenges.

We all get tangled, and we all get snagged. When dealing with an especially problematic snarl, it can sometimes be a difficult to decide whether time would be better spent simply cutting-loose and rerigging, versus making the continued efforts to extricate oneself from a particularly troublesome rat's nest. I don't have a hard-and-fast rule for this one; I suppose one needs to weigh the overall value of the current setup and see if they feel it's worth salvaging.

More often than not, if things have gotten too messy, it's likely a wise course of action to start fresh—perhaps making some positive adjustments to one's rig in the process.

As for snags, I think I'd go so far as to say that—if you *AREN'T* getting hung-up from time to time—you're probably not doing your best fishing. Risk avoidance is fine, to a point, but the biggest fish are often found close to the bottom, directly under that problematic sweeper, or hugging tightly to the bank under a canopy of overhanging alder. You'll never catch the big ones if you aren't fishing where they're holding, and you need to have the courage to put your best efforts out there. You'll likely lose a fly from time to time, but you need to ask yourself the following question: Why are you even out there, if not to try and catch the nicest fish possible?

KEEPING THE DRIFT GOING

While I'm definitely not ready to take up the rocking chair yet, I'm already at a point where I can start evaluating certain aspects of my life with a bit more perspective and objectivity. It's funny, but I can now easily categorize almost every component of my life within the framework of my angler's philosophy. Spending time with people? Make sure they're good friends, with little need for extraneous drama. Getting married? Do it once, with the right type of partner. Choosing a career? Find something that allows for meaning and purpose, with some fun and excitement thrown in. Staying in the North? Build a place above the ice-fog, revel in the freedom from crowds and traffic, and enjoy the unique aspects delivered by all the seasons.

As I said before, I certainly don't claim to have everything completely figured out.

However, I'm confident that my flyfisher's perspective has served me quite well thus far. There are too many things in life that can potentially drag one in unwanted directions, and I've learned to recognize the mend-points pretty well. Problems and challenges will inevitably continue to arise from time to time, but I feel I'm standing on a relatively firm streambank. There's not much that seems to be either pushing or pulling me in an unwanted fashion at this point, and the path of my ongoing drift looks pretty good to me. ◉

Chapter Sixteen

TRUE CATCH-AND-RELEASE:
Seizing Gratitude, and Letting Go
of Self-Imposed Limitations

It has been many years since I killed a trout—or a grayling, for that matter. Wild fish inhabiting free-flowing streams are a precious resource, and it can take a disproportionally long time for them to amass any sufficient bulk while plying the waters of the Far North. Some of the streams that I fish can be reached by the road, whereas others are only accessible by air.

However—even for those drainages appearing to be "remote" when viewing the largely untracked map of Alaska—the reach of the floatplane is far indeed. The value of any native fish lies far beyond its immediate caloric value, as they can bestow the gift of their treasured existence on a repeating and continuous basis, provided that anglers treat them with the utmost care and respect.

When it comes to freshwater salmonids, I've been a strict catch-and-release fisherman for quite some time. This made for some interesting conversation and debate early on in my marriage; my wife Gwendolyn is an Alaskan Native, specifically a Deg Hit'an Athabascan Indian, whose peoples traditionally inhabited the lower stretches of the Yukon River country in and around the village of Holy Cross. I often tease her that she's supposed to be a "person of the land," as the approach of a mosquito (or any other insect within close proximity) sends her into a state of near apoplexy. However, when it comes to Gwen's preferred sources of caloric intake, it's clear that her genetic rivers run deep.

We don't buy red meat in the store; a yearly moose—or my half-share thereof—will sustain us handily, with the bulk of our annual bounty being ground into burger for many of our preferred meals. I used to take a moose nearly every year, even managing a few with a bow in the management area that surrounds our home. When my primary hunting partner retired and left Alaska to move south, I went through a bit of a dry spell as I worked to configure new arrangements. Gwen was never too pushy about it, but there were more than a few comments made as the supply of meat in our freezer began to dwindle. I've now managed to link up with a new partner—one who fulfills the requisite "hunting friend" criteria addressed in an earlier chapter. Our freezer has once again maintained a steady supply of moose for the past few years, contributing to the overall harmony of the household.

We alternate the rotation of our protein with that of salmon—most commonly the Copper River sockeye that we net every summer outside of Chitina. The State of Alaska manages a personal-use dipnet fishery on the Copper, allowing every resident "head of household" to scoop up thirty salmon from the river's churning, silt-laden waters for their yearly consumption. Limits are expanded during years of strong runs, and one (considerably larger) king salmon can be retained during years where their escapement totals have been reached.

Gwen is a fairly diminutive person, with a beautiful smile and somewhat reserved disposition. However, once she's started to dipnet for fish and gets that feverish, sockeye-tinged gleam in her eyes, one doesn't want to mess with her. For her, fish are food—and rightly so. I don't think twice about taking our yearly allotment of salmon, as it's part of a well-managed, sustainable resource plan. Yearly quotas are set by management biologists who monitor the overall health of the fishery, and the harvest is promptly shut down if it appears there's any danger of escapement targets not being met.

We'll usually receive some additional salmon—often smoked strips of Yukon River king—from some of Gwen's extended family. The kings that are bound for locations far up the Yukon incorporate an exceptional amount of oil into their flesh, as their journey could potentially take them as far as Canada. It's this high oil-content that gives the Yukon king its particularly rich flavor, categorizing the bestowment of any smoked offering as a highly prized gift. If you thought that messing with my wife's Copper River red was a bad idea, you *definitely* don't want to be caught pilfering from her bag of Yukon strips . . .

Back in the early 90s, when Gwen and I first started dating, I brought her with me to fish the Anchor River for steelhead and dollies on Alaska's Kenai Peninsula. I would soon discover that her considered opinion of my primary avocation in life—to include my strict, catch-and-release ethic, basically amounted to "playing with one's food." I'll give her credit—she was quite the good sport in the brand-new neoprenes and wading boots I'd purchased for her, and she managed to bring in several nice dolly varden on a flyrod once we'd located a pod of feeders. However, the look of complete shock and betrayal upon her face when I carefully unhooked and released her first fish is one that I'll likely never forget.

Gwen doesn't stream-fish with me very often these days, and that's okay. She'll normally do quite well when we do go out, though she's usually content to simply enjoy the day's float, pick berries, or take photographs while I concentrate on my fishing. I'm pretty sure that she still finds most of my non-consumptive endeavors to be somewhat silly, though she certainly understands the necessity for catch-and-release management in places like Katmai and other high-use drainages when it comes to trout and char. As is the case with many other areas in our life, we've reached a comfortable level of drag-free drift, often taking our small motorhome to road-based fisheries where I can hike-off to fish for the day, while she stays in the camper and performs her exquisite bead-work in warm (and bug-free) conditions of relative comfort.

The difference in Gwen's and my outlooks on certain things doesn't alarm me; in most cases they actually cause me to examine my own self-imposed limitations, in an effort to see whether I've inadvertently veered off the tracks somewhere. More often than not it comes down to a simple difference in perspectives, with no significant adjustment required on either of our parts. As the husband, I'm sure that one of these days I'll find that I was indeed proven right on some major issue; if and when that happens, I may issue an updated, special edition of this book, just to ensure that everyone has been made aware of my amended track record.

As my readers can hopefully tell, I'm actually having quite a bit of fun living my life these days. As I continued to take pleasure in the increased level of perspective that comes with a bit of age, I've also been pondering a question that's been slowly percolating in my mind. It's somewhat of a "chicken-or-egg" kind of thing, though for the purposes of this book I suppose a "fish-or-egg" comparison would make far more sense. Anyway, the inquiry I've posed to myself is this: *Has the fishing that I've enjoyed over the years been made better because of the life that I've led, or has my life been made better by virtue of the fact that I'm a fisherman?* In the end, I suppose it probably doesn't make much of a difference- but after giving it a significant amount of thought, I'm more inclined to ascribe to the latter.

I've spoken several times to the importance of having a "fisher-man's perspective," and this has proven to be true across a multitude of situations and circumstances in my own life. I spent the significant majority of my working career supervising others, and it was through many of these interactions that I realized just how disadvantaged some poor souls can be when they don't have the benefit of an angler's experience in life. God bless HR people, but their rigidity and adherence to strict process oftentimes killed me. When setting-up or sitting on a hiring board I would often want to craft a fishing-related question, to gauge the comparative analytical approaches across a selection of candidates. Invariably, I would be told that such questions were not "specifically job-related or task-specific and should thus be refrained from." Hmphhh . . . if someone's not smart enough to know when another split-shot is obviously needed, that's a piece of information that I want to know.

I actually spoke with my dad about this a few times, as he was heavily involved in personnel management throughout the course of his career as well. He readily agreed with my assessment, speaking to the various caliber of people that he had met through fishing—particularly those at fly-fishing venues—versus those met elsewhere. It doesn't necessarily seem to be a matter of mere preference through shared-interests; rather, there truly *does* seem to be some type of "special formula" that gets hard-wired into the brains of dedicated fly fishermen, with an inevitable spillover component that transfers to the rest of their lives. While it might not meet HR rules, if I had to hire from within a group of candidates where all other factors were equal—and the position required an exceptional degree of forethought, independent judgement, and analytical flexibility—I'd hire the competent flyfisher every time.

As I continue to find both joy and meaning in my flyfisher's perspective, I'm invariably led back to feelings of profound thankfulness, as well as recognizing some of the extraordinary strokes of luck that have helped to shape my existence. While the task of mending a fly line can reinforce the illusion that one's in complete control of their own destiny, such a conclusion would be highly disingenuous. I had no say in the matter regarding which family I'd be born into; nor did I exert any influence in my parent's chosen fields of interest. My father could've just as easily decided to pack up and move his young family to Los Angeles or Dallas; the mere possibility of such an alternate reality chills me to a far greater extent than any Fairbanks winter ever could.

If I'd ended up at a different high school in Anchorage, I'd have likely never met Willy, Dave, and Glen. Dave's stepdad would've never factored into my life, and the door that opened to Katmai might've remained closed to me forever. Attending the University of Alaska in Fairbanks led to a life spent in the Interior, where a solid career, amazing wife, and a perfect stretch of home-water all awaited discovery. The extended length of our winters can indeed be a bit trying at times, but when I look at everything on-balance, it's more than worth it.

When I reflect on the many different components that comprise our life here in Alaska, I'm often overwhelmed by a sense of both humbled awe, and extraordinary gratitude. It can be too easy to take things for granted at times, and—especially here—one can easily become desensitized to the profound beauty that surrounds us on a daily basis. As a kid, my mother would frequently remind all of us kids to count our blessings—and to this day I endeavor to retain my sense of wonder.

"Blessings" . . . it's an interesting word. Received within the context of my mother's religious admonitions, it carried a context of divine bestowment—where specific benefits were theoretically being sent down from a mysterious man in the clouds. I have my own thoughts as to the origins of this world's most divine circumstances, though none of these differences diminish their significance or overall worth in the slightest degree. While my own conception or use of the word may carry a slightly different connotation, I don't hesitate to use it. I recognize that I have indeed been blessed to an amazing degree, and any failure to acknowledge this abundance of gifts would constitute the closest thing to a true "sin" that I can conceive, in accordance with the archival definitions of my past.

In the previous chapter, I spoke to the fact that my dad isn't on social media, and that I often must create duplicate communications to send to him via regular email. While I forward him a fair amount of stuff on a regular basis, I'll rarely get an electronic reply. Dad seems to save most of his conversational fodder for our weekly Sunday phone calls, and that's just fine with me.

This past year, while going through a box of several years' worth of photos to scan into computer storage, I ran across a couple of really nice ones—one of me with my dad in a boat along the banks of the Kulik River, and the other showing Mom and I, fly rods in hand, standing alongside a stretch of the Gunnison's Lake Fork. I suppose I must've been feeling somewhat nostalgic that day, as I incorporated both photos into a simple Facebook post, declaring: "One of the most profound blessings experienced in my life: TO HAVE BEEN RAISED BY PARENTS WHO FISHED." I later figured that Dad might appreciate the sentiment as well, so I casually pasted a screen-snip of the post into an email that I'd already prepared to send him.

Two or three days later—I can't really remember which—I opened my email to find a message from Dad waiting in my inbox. To receive an electronic note from him was somewhat of a rarity in and of itself, and I wasn't surprised to find that it appeared to be quite short upon opening it. The message was a single sentence in its entirety, as it simply said,

> *"Danny—Your note was the single greatest piece of communication that I have ever received.*
> *Love—Pop."*

I think I may have cried just a little bit that day. ◉

About the Author

After completing his stint as a fly-fishing guide in Katmai, Daniel graduated from the University of Alaska with a degree in Wildlife Biology. He then shifted gears to begin a career in law enforcement, ultimately serving 20 years with the Fairbanks Police Department where he retired as Chief of Police in 2009. Daniel spent the following decade supervising corporate risk and security functions in the private sector before leaving to start his own consultancy business, addressing organizational risk management, crisis preparations, and emergency communications.

Remaining in Fairbanks as a nearly lifelong Alaskan with his wife Gwendolyn, Daniel has tailored the delivery of his planning and preparatory service to address the needs of Alaska-based businesses; he particularly enjoys serving facilities based in remote locations, far from emergency response resources.

When he's not fishing, writing, or engaged in other work, Daniel enjoys public speaking, addressing business groups and discussing the challenges inherent in developing sound risk management practices, crisis management plans and procedures, and topics associated with leadership development and personal growth. Reflecting the principles in this book, Dan tends to deliver his presentations within the framework of the flyfisher's perspective, ideally suited for corporate retreats at fishing-related venues. For those interested in contacting Daniel, visit Hoffman Consulting at: **https://hoffmanready.com**